Spin Between
Never and Ever

Spin Between
Never and Ever

Shannon C. Flynn

To order additional copies of this book, contact:
Xlibris Corporation
1-888-795-4274
www.Xlibris.com
Orders@Xlibris.com
86217

I dedicate this book to my parents and brothers and sisters who loved and supported me through my initial illness and efforts to recover;

And to my husband, whose nurturance and belief in me helps me back to recovery when I struggle in the present

PENDULUM

Lonely, I look out my window:
Dizzying dazzle of stars.
Through falling crystal the wind sweeps in waves,
Sounding in synchronicity,
Webbing the night with music.

Spin between never and ever—
Which future will come to pass?
Riding the pendulum's waxing and waning,
Inner and outer space I cleave.
Do I leave any footprints?

Gentle blue light of the full moon
Still cannot shield me from shadows.
Cavernous chaos and treacherous time—
When will I see the morning?
Will I ever see the morning?

—Poem/song written about bipolar disorder while in college (circa 1989)

Why are my dreams never realized?
Why do my brightest hopes fade?
Why do my fantasies all turn to dust?
Lost in life's tears and blindness, yes,
Lost in life's tears and blindness.

—Poem/song to the same tune written at age 12 (circa 1979)

FOREWORD

When my sister Shannon first told me that she had penned her memoirs, I was thoroughly intrigued. Having been born four years younger, I always looked up to Shannon throughout my childhood. From the very start of my formative years, Shannon stood within our ever-expanding family at the apex of achievement, presenting the quintessential model of perfect behavior, educational excellence, and extracurricular ambition.

Given that past, the insight her memoirs would provide, about the discipline behind her flawless record of achievement and the motivations that fuel such perfection, could only enhance my personal pursuits as I progress through my own adult life.

But the intrigue that compelled my first reading of her memoirs was much more than a desire to parse the awe that Shannon had inspired in most of her siblings throughout our youth. And indeed the essence of her story is of far greater value to society at large, than a simple examination of a straight A student. For while Shannon's story does partially chronicle the rigors of that "perfect child" facade which adorned her early life, the whole of that now seems almost insignificant by comparison to what followed.

From my perspective at that time, Shannon's early life died in one single afternoon that I will never forget during her senior year of high school. That life was destroyed by a set of circumstances and events that heretofore I have only barely understood. To me, at the time, those events seemed utterly abrupt and cruelly irreversible. They were staggering as much in their destruction of the Shannon that I knew, as in their apparently ineluctable demolition of the rest of her life.

The shadowy assassin that preyed on her poise and happiness, that forever altered the landscape of her life and our family's concept of well being, was mental illness. These memoirs are the story of Shannon's desperate struggles with a disease that visits daily misery upon unnumbered victims across the world, in the forms of depression and bipolar disorder.

Shannon suffered both of these illnesses, to an extent that I have never fully grasped and with a quiet desperation that I never truly even detected. This is her story of facing her illness, of dealing with its terrible symptoms both urgent and enduring, and of emerging from that morass with a sense of self that is at once altogether altered and eternally renewable.

It is a story of triumph unlike any other I have ever encountered. This, to me, is the essential instruction manual on how to be happy.

Make no mistake: this is a brutally honest account of a haunted existence that roiled for many years in relentless melancholy. It is stark in its honesty, and even frightening in parts. It imposes a distinct measure of revulsion in certain sections, through its meticulous description of what it really means in this day and age to be mentally ill.

And it was indeed these passages that provided for me the insights I had been wanting since first confronting the reality that my sister Shannon was not in fact perfect. The ponderous weight of mental illness is distributed across any support structure that a victim is fortunate to have, and our family was both larger than average and fairly tight-knit. But when I first reckoned with the truth that her world was far from idyllic, that she was in fact deeply troubled and not in total control, it threw my own world off its axis in a rippling effect that reverberated throughout our whole family.

And it inevitably prompted questions that were simply never answered in advance of this memoir's emergence. For me, and I'm sure for so many people trapped in the frustration of wanting to help a mentally ill loved one, the literature that follows holds tremendous value in deconstructing the veil of mystery that outwardly obfuscates any personal struggle against mental illness.

For this story is at its core an examination of the ruthless acuity with which mental illness targets its individual victims, and the appalling efficiency with which it isolates them inside a separate reality that others so often cannot even perceive, much less penetrate. Shannon's frank discussion of the basic mechanics and far-reaching influences of depression and bipolar disorder will certainly resonate with those who have endured mental illness, and illuminate all else who have observed its effects on its victims. This account is, therefore, an important examination of the pathos of a ravaging disease.

But this story is also an incredible exposition of strength and hope, and the redemption that is available to anyone who works hard to achieve their goals, even while sacrificing long-held dreams. It is a beautiful essay not of a life destroyed or potential lost, but of promise preserved and innocence saved. It is the unbending assertion that this precious existence we all share is a luminous vessel of extraordinary intrinsic value, no matter the state of the ocean it floats on.

This story is, in short, a love letter to life. Shannon's essential qualities – her humility, her grace, and her continuing poise that has endured throughout all of the awful experiences - emerge in this account as if unscathed. These qualities emanate from Shannon's memoirs exactly as I remember them from her youth, burgeoning forth from unbridled enthusiasm and steeped in happy awe toward the simple joys of being alive.

This is the essence of Shannon's story: enthusiasm and awe for simply being alive. It is indeed a story of triumph unlike any other I have ever read, and I recommend it to any audience with the pride of a younger brother who benefitted so momentously, just by providing witness.

-J. Patrick Flynn
25 October 2010

INTRODUCTION:
FROM THE ABYSS TO RECOVERY

I hunched at my school desk, 17 and slipping into an abyss whose shadow I had barely glimpsed before. My left hand shook with free-associations in a spatter of words that galloped through my head and outside the margins of lined notebook paper.

"Dark, it's so dark—like it was night even though it's 8:00 in the morning—Warning: Everything's going to fall fall apart my heart will break and take away everything my mind is fading fast fast vast emptiness oh help the universe is coming to get me . . . "

My mind whirled and then faded, dead inside, into a suffocating fog. Speaking of "dead"—that was all I wanted. Well, it wasn't that I *wanted* to die; I *had* to. I needed to escape the tumult that was exhausting my emotional and physical resources. And I had to die because I deserved to, because I was evil. I knew that I had transformed absolutely into a rotten core.

I had recently discovered this one horrifying night when it became clear as I raced around my bedroom that I was the reincarnation of Judas Iscariot, betrayer of Jesus. And I would plunge to hell like he had, so why shouldn't I kill myself now to get it over with? Especially since I was only a burden to everyone around me. My family and friends would rejoice once I was dead.

These thoughts progressed to the point that I could no longer touch anyone, so that I would not contaminate them with my toxic essence. Then I could no longer allow my fingers or limbs to touch each other, because somehow this was evil, too. Soon God no longer permitted me to eat or sleep because I was such a monstrosity. I stopped showering and changing clothes, almost stopped speaking.

Within six or eight weeks I was no longer able to attend high school. My days shrunk to merely huddling on a chair in our living room, guarded by my parents and siblings in shifts. Every moment I could snatch to myself, I punched holes in my wrist with a safety pin hidden in my sleeve.

One afternoon, left alone for a minute, I crept furtively to the top of the second-floor flight of stairs, about to hurl myself down them—until I was discovered and tugged back downstairs, held tightly by the hand.

Finally my mind and body were so clamped down by dark gravity that I was no longer able to hurt myself. One day I simply goggled at the unfamiliar face in our cold bathroom mirror. *Who is that? I'm not me anymore . . . I'm an alien,* I decided. *Someone or something has stolen my identity and taken me over. Well, it can have me—I surrender because I am worth nothing anyway. So nothing matters. I certainly don't matter.*

During those gray hours, days, and months, my mind cramped into nothing but ruminations of worthlessness, and I didn't matter to myself at all. Luckily, of course to my parents and brothers and sisters I did matter, very much. Even if they puzzled over what was happening to me as much as I did, they intuited my distress and incapacitation, and they got me help. My family brought me to a psychiatric hospital, where I stayed for a month. I was diagnosed with depression with psychotic features, and was given antidepressants and an antipsychotic. While in the hospital, I discovered art therapy and painted surreal abstracts and wrote long narrative poems about my depression and recovery. And recover I did, into the blessed contentment of feeling like myself again—a brighter, happier self at that.

Now, armed with a name for what ailed me, I consumed volumes about depression and bipolar disorder. I devoured books and articles about psychotropic medications and art therapy and theories of psychiatric rehabilitation and mood charting and the consumer movement. (Many users of mental health services refer to themselves as "consumers." The consumer movement is consumers working together to advocate and make change in the mental health system and in society.) I discovered Kay Redfield Jamison, Ph.D., who became a role model, and pored over her memoir, *An Unquiet Mind,* as well as *Manic-Depressive Illness,* the authoritative text on bipolar disorder that Jamison wrote with Frederick Goodwin, M.D. I involved myself with one of the nation's leading mental health advocacy organizations, the National Alliance on Mental Illness (NAMI) and 12 years later would assume a leadership role on its Consumer Council as well as training people to lead consumer support groups. While serving on the NAMI Consumer Council, I befriended another role model, Suzanne Vogel-Scibilia, M.D., a psychiatrist who also is a consumer living with bipolar disorder and the married mother to five children. Later I read Martha Manning's *Undercurrents* and Patty Duke's *Call Me Anna.* And a pamphlet produced by the National Institute of Mental Health (NIMH, part of the

National Institutes of Health in Bethesda, MD), about bipolar disorder, the "kindling effect," circadian rhythms, and mood cycles, fascinated me.

Little did I know then, in the just-thawed winter of my senior year in high school, that my wellness journey would lead me to a college degree in psychology. Then a master's degree in art therapy. And a post-master's certificate in mental health counseling and plans for an eventual doctorate in psychology. And a career that has included helping people with psychiatric conditions heal through art therapy and counseling, as well as 20 years of work at the very organization that had produced the leaflet that had so intrigued me, the NIMH itself, where I would assist with research into the genetics of schizophrenia and recruit patients for non-invasive studies concerning that illness.

As well, the more time passes since my first episode, the more I realize that my illness—which has evolved from depression to bipolar disorder with generalized anxiety disorder—is not my identity. I used to say "I am mentally ill" but the truth demands that I say "I have a mental illness." And realism and relativity give way to "I am Shannon Flynn, a multifaceted person—like everyone else on the planet—who just happens to live with mental health issues." As I started working with clients with devastated lives, hard-won insight led me to grasp that I'm not the only one who's ever suffered! Lots of people have more agonizing crosses to bear than I could ever fathom. Life really isn't always fair.

This realization leads me to one of the chief reasons I wrote this book. If even one person who reads this memoir sees herself or himself in the struggles I've faced, then perhaps I've educated that person or inspired her or him to find help. I also want to show people who may not believe in their own power to heal that it is possible to recover and live successfully with a psychiatric illness.

As well, I aim to reduce the stigma of mental illness by adding my voice to those of others who have chronicled their stories in some form of media. The incidence of bipolar disorder is estimated to be 1% to 5%, perhaps more. Some 10% or more of us suffer from depression, and schizophrenia affects 1 in 100 Americans. And in the general American public, one in four to one in five of us will experience some sort of psychiatric problem during our lives! Mental illness touches one in every four families in the United States—clearly, the time to talk about it openly is long overdue.

So many pieces fit into the landscape puzzle of my recovery: my psychiatrists' and psychotherapists' superb care in helping me through counseling and medicine; my art and writing; my spirituality and conception of God; meaningful full-time work; the support of my family and friends; and especially, in recent years, the enduring love of my husband Tom. All of these pieces shape the hope that shows me how to return, and return again, to being myself. They afford me self-knowledge that allows me to better predict and control my mood swings. Achieving some measure of well-being continues to fuel my passion to improve the well-being of those who live with similar illnesses. It leads me toward wholeness, that I may help others become more whole as well. And that to my mind is true recovery.

THE EARLY BEGINNINGS

I spent the first 10 years of my life in a cozy neighborhood within the city of Lancaster, PA, in the south-central part of the state. The area was mostly white, mostly blue collar. I was the first born in a family of 12 kids (seven adopted)—my father ("Ned") was an accountant and my mother ("Betty") worked at a nonprofit advocacy organization. We were generally a happy, secure, middle-class family. But unfolding the narrative of my life starts with a much less idyllic fact: I've lived probably my entire life with what used to be called "depressive personality disorder" and would now be considered dysthymia.

As a child I characteristically looked on the dark side of life, expecting always to be punished for my (sometimes imagined) flaws and misdeeds. I believed these reprimands would come not only from God, but also from my parents. I have a vivid memory of sheltering under my bed every morning during the summer of my fifth year, to hide from the spankings I "knew" would be meted out to me. That they never actually occurred did not seem sufficient cause to stop hiding. I've had such early childhood memories challenged by parents or siblings, so that I now believe that my depression colored my perspective, enough to distort my recall of what actually happened to me. (And rather than villains, my parents were actually loving and supportive. I can reflect now that my fear of punishment and self-hate were born of my depression, not my home environment.)

Still, I do remember that hating myself was second nature throughout my childhood, adolescence, and early adulthood. I typically viewed myself as an automatic member of a lower caste than everyone else around me. If I was in a group of friends and we numbered, say, five, I would be surprised when one girl would count us off to figure out how many movie tickets to ask for, and she counted five. I had half-thought I was invisible and shouldn't actually be counted.

Was I different even then, as a six-year-old child who was too afraid to play the game by the rules? Was I in fact ever "normal"?

The "game" in question was all the rage among our first-grade class at recess and would continue ad infinitum with little variation. It was simple (not to mention sexist): all the girls would crouch together, giggling, in a gravel pit in the far corner of the playground. Then, at a signal from the boy "guarding" the pit, the girls would all flee, laughing, to be caught by the boys and "thrown" back into the pit, only to escape again when the guard wasn't looking. Except for me.

"One . . . two . . . three! We're gonna get you, we're gonna get you!" the gaggle of boys crowed.

"Eeek! Oh no!" yelped one of the girls.

"Run away, quick! I don't want those dumb boys catching me!" squealed another.

"Come on, Shannon, you run away too! Or they'll catch you . . ."—yet another little girl.

"Nah, let her alone. Everyone knows she never runs. She just stays in the pit," scorned the boy "guard."

And I did just stay in the gravel pit, brooding over why I wasn't a better person. Whether I was good, moral, and humble enough preoccupied me constantly. The pious doctrines of the nuns and priests at our Catholic school and church that didn't seem to bother my brothers and sisters overly much struck terror into my heart. For hours I read children's books about saints and martyrs and contemplated all those who'd been burned at the stake, had body parts lopped off, or submitted to murder rather than lose their maidenly virtue. *I'm not nearly as holy as they were,* I reasoned, *so I deserve those horrible things much more. What if God is even now plotting my death by beheading, fire, or fatal gunshot wound?* It became my quest—one I've never completely abandoned since—to be Perfect.

If I could just attain—and maintain—perfection, then no one could get angry at me: not my teachers, not my parents, not even God. People stopped loving you when they became angry—I knew that intuitively. (And I'm only now learning that just because someone close to you gets angry, it doesn't diminish the love between you.)

Naturally, I shrunk back in social situations outside of my immediate family. On the first day of first grade, I crept into the noisy, crowded cafeteria and cringed instantly with overwhelm from the human stimuli impinging on my truly "nervous" system. From then on through third grade, I ate lunch every day at home, trotting with shallow breaths of relief the two blocks back to my house and to the comfort of my mother, come noontime.

Though exceedingly shy and anxious, I struggled at once with pridefulness that led me to expect superhuman accomplishments of myself. I stretched on tiptoes toward impossibly high standards of outward behavior and even inward thoughts, so it should have come as no surprise that I continually failed to meet them. Yet I berated myself harshly for such failures: *Shannon, you ninny, why didn't you get 100 on every single spelling quiz this year? Why did that other girl get more compliments on her painting than you did on yours? You're so messed up. Everybody hates you, and I hate you most.*

Over-seriousness, perfectionism, and self-denigration to the point of actually hating myself at times—all of these traits were mixed in me with a near-grandiose opinion of my intelligence, artistic abilities, and leadership skills. The oldest child in a large family that would eventually include 11 brothers and sisters, I also was a scholar who had been taught by my loving and patient mother to read at the age of four. I was an extraordinarily diligent student who toiled for hours over homework, even in elementary school. I also read any book I could get my hands on, straining my eyes by moonlight to fill my mind with just one more paragraph, just one more page, long after my mom told my sisters and me to turn off our light at night.

With a strange blend of arrogance and debasement, I cried every time I fell short of an A+ grade, shaken at once with disgust over my "defeat" and "mistakes" and astonishment that I had in fact not measured up to my yardstick. (The paramount importance of obtaining straight As has dogged me throughout my academic career, all the way through graduate school.) My devoted parents never failed to affirm my intelligence and creativity; I began to ruminate anxiously over whether I was "humble" enough. I occasionally—though not as often as I knew I should—began sleeping on stacks of hardcover books on the floor instead of on pillows in my warm bed. My petty kid's quarrels with my many brothers and sisters I tried mightily to squelch, convincing myself that being "invisible" through virtuous non-confrontation was the only way to shrug off my irrational dread. I also took up the habit, at least at home, of murmuring to myself about how well I was living up to my own and God's expectations.

A vivid memory from my third year of catechism class haunts me to this day: in a religion class the nun taught us the story of Abraham and Isaac in the Old Testament. I chilled, listening in horror as she intoned, "Remember, boys and girls, God told Abraham to kill his own son to show that he loved God. And Abraham loved God so much that he was willing to do this; Isaac, his son, loved God enough to be willing to die. Isn't their obedience and dedication wonderful?"

Nowadays, a compassionate clergy member might interpret this parable as a sign of the loving bond between God and Abraham, and of God's mercy in sparing Abraham from slaying his son. Then (in 1975), however, the nun sternly informed us eight-year-olds that the moral of this Bible story was that *at any time* God might expect us to submit to death to prove we loved Him, and that we must all be ready to do so. *Oh no,* I thought. *It's just as I suspected—God is planning to punish me for my sins.*

Looking back, I wonder if I even heard that nun correctly—or whether my quasi-delusional depression once again spilled a black wash over my memory of her lesson. Regardless of whether the events I recall truly happened, my interpretation of that moment imbued me with a lasting sense of impending doom. My instinct of reacting fearfully to events rather than acting confidently in the world has persisted to this day. Perhaps I am one of Jerome Kagan's hypothesized "highly reactive" babies grown up. (Kagan is a pioneer of HYPERLINK "http://en.wikipedia.org/wiki/Developmental_psychology" \o "Developmental psychology" *developmental psychology*; his studies on "reactivity" of temperament led him to label as highly reactive the child with an inborn temperament that was anxious, difficult to sooth, and easily worried.)

Hearing this tale of God's almighty wrath may have contributed to my first attempts to hurt myself, at the age of eight. I remember one summer day getting upset because a teasing neighborhood boy informed me gleefully that "Someday you'll get married—then you can make babies!" and leering at me through our shared (though extremely vague) knowledge of what "making babies" entailed. I was so humiliated by his suggestive remarks (even though both he and I barely knew what he was suggesting) that I couldn't reply but instead fled around to the side of the house to slam my head against the outside brick wall. As I did so, I inchoately realized that, yes, this hurt—but it distracted me from the disturbing implications of what the little boy had said. And this technique, however malignant, was so effective that I only made the connection between my first instance of self-harm and the boy's remarks about sex *as I wrote this paragraph.* The physical pain must have buried the association in my unconscious.

From then on I relied on the practice of banging my head on the wall or shattering favorite possessions, such as the prized crystal rabbit given me by my godfather, whenever emotional pain or cognitive discomfort loomed. I doubt that my parents fully knew that I hurt myself to that degree; with as many as 11 other kids in the house to deal with, my behavior probably slipped under the radar.

I also remember reading *Little Women* and despairing of ever being as sweet and uncomplaining (even in death) as was Beth March. *What's wrong with me?* I asked myself. *Beth threw her mittens out the window to poor children. Beth gave up her breakfast so the poor kids could have something to eat. I'm just too selfish to do that.* These failings I confessed shamefully to the parish priest on Saturdays. Given an injunction to pray "three Our Fathers and two Hail Marys" as penance, I scrupulously asked myself why he hadn't drawn back in disgust at my sinfulness instead and ordered me to enter a convent immediately.

My perfectionism persisted into sixth grade, when I competed with the seventh and eighth graders in our parochial school spelling bee. To my delight, I won the school bee—which also won me ownership of the coveted "Praying Hands" sculpture (luridly painted, not glazed) that our art teacher had created—and advanced to our city spelling contest. I dutifully won that spelling bee, according to plan, and was slated to compete in the county spelling bee. The winner of that competition would go on to the national spelling bee, a contest I dreadfully wanted to win. On the fateful night, in the packed town hall auditorium, I advanced to round after round against children from across the county.

Only three of us remained onstage when I was asked to spell the word "savant." I knew what the word meant, having secretly hoped and wondered whether I would ever meet the qualifications to be one. But apparently I was not a savant, for I stupidly spelled the word "savvant" (reasoning that it would be spelled similarly to the related word "savvy") and was promptly disqualified. I exited the stage in tears and after the contest hung my head in shame upon reuniting with my parents, siblings, and school friends who had gathered to see my moment of "triumph." *Hah,* I thought angrily—*some savant I am.*

My mom gamely tried to comfort me, telling me gently that when she had been in elementary school, she too had competed in spelling bees and had won third place in a county bee. I think she was trying to stress the idea that I had "won," but I fixated on the hard fact that third place just didn't cut it, at least not as far as I was concerned. I had disappointed not only myself, but also my whole family *and* my entire school. My dream was over; I was not the best anymore. In my warped black-and-white value system, not to be the absolute best was to be the absolute worst.

And in the social arena, obviously I remained interpersonally stuck at the age of my depressive prodrome, the early teens, for quite a long time. This helps explain why I simply couldn't navigate through the adolescent routines of flirting and dating, which were taken for granted by my smoother peers. My social awkwardness also was reinforced by my innate introversion and my quasi-psychotic oddness. And as I grew older, my reticence and strange behavior if anything intensified along with my perfectionism. Although I could shine in small groups of close girl friends, around the popular cliques of kids and at parties, I cringed in corners. Literally.

This behavior first emerged at a co-ed dance to celebrate our eighth-grade graduation. During the party, a very bright 13-year-old boy I respected and secretly "liked" asked me to dance. I was so flummoxed by the invitation, and by the fear that others would know of my interest in him, that I turned him down with a stutter. I then proceeded to sit under a table in the far recesses of the gym and mutter to myself anxiously about this troubling situation! Needless to say, the boy did not seek me out again.

As well, the unattainable goal of excelling at everything I attempted accounts for much of my pre-morbid adolescent fixation with becoming a famous actress once I finished high school and college. I was once told that at the age of seven or eight, I was a "take-charge lady" because I was constantly drawing, creating stories, and writing plays that I more or less forced my brothers and sisters to act in, naturally reserving the leading roles for myself. At the time, I had no doubt that I would be a famous artist, singer, or actress "when I grew up."

My creative activities and desire for recognition also highlight the fact that my childhood, despite the way I've described it thus far, was by no means uniformly miserable. I frequently enjoyed playing with my brothers and sisters and teaching them to read; swimming with friends in the community pool during long, mild Pennsylvania summers; and checking out as many books as I could carry home from the Lancaster city library.

Nevertheless, in junior high and high school, I held fast to my unattainable standards along with my off-and-on strangeness, constantly comparing myself with my sisters and classmates who had similar abilities as did I. I had a similarly conflicted relationship with one of my sisters ("Ellen") as a teenager. As genetics would have it, we developed very similar interests and talents: theater, vocal music, and creative writing. Many times I inwardly cursed her for getting the poetry award, the solo in the choir, or the role in the school play that I had coveted. Because I was an angst-ridden teenager and because in my moodiness my whole life seemed a bitter melodrama, I didn't merely half-heartedly wish I'd gotten the award or part instead. No, I actively loathed my sister for her win, and often banged my head over and over again in anger. And my hapless sister, guilty of nothing more than progressing through the teen years normally, suffered needlessly for my pride and anger that exacerbated ordinary sibling rivalry. I also frequently decided that I "hated" various young women in my high school classes for what I shamefully considered their superior talents, when the person I really hated was myself for not measuring up to the others' performances.

Above all, though, I've never been able to bear knowing that someone surpassed me in intelligence—I still have a difficult time controlling my inner rage when I encounter a person who clearly outperforms me in that arena. The driving force behind my storms of jealousy and hatred has been the irrational conviction that no one, including me, will be able to love me if I am not the very best at everything. It is as though I need to prove my worthiness to myself and to the important people in my life. It is never enough simply to be Shannon; I must be the uber-Shannon—and I've lived long enough to realize I never will be, nor can be, that person. One of these days I'll realize that all I need to be is myself; surely the abiding love of my husband and family and friends should convince me of this, but violent fluctuation is the very nature of bipolar self-confidence.

Another of my girlhood convictions, which strengthened as I entered my teenage years and found myself dateless time and again: God had finally handed down judgment, punishing me for being so evil by arranging my life such that I would never have a date or get married but instead would have to be a nun. The reason I never dated until the age of 19 or was even kissed for the first time until I was 20 seems obvious now: my near-psychotic intensity and neediness scared the boys away. But back then, I watched my sisters—my *younger* sisters, no less—go on dates and to parties with angry envy. I sang along to my radio playing the oldies station, to the wistful old Janis Ian song about "ugly duckling girls at 17" who were fated to be alone. My lot lay with them, I knew.

Once again, I'm the odd one out. My sisters get to date boys and go to the homecoming dance while I'm stuck with babysitting the neighbor kids and studying once they're asleep. Thanks a lot, God, for making me have to be a nun when I'm an adult, instead of getting married like a normal *person would. Not that anyone would mistake me for normal . . .*

So many times I lamented my awkward social reserve, watching one or another of my sisters and friends effortlessly wear makeup, flirt with and go out with boys—even, once, the same boy I had my heart set on. It took several months for me to forgive my friend for "stealing" the young man I had been attracted to—when she never set out to do so. He just happened to prefer her, and my predictable reaction was hysterical, hateful envy. I was given to singling out girls who were, as I saw it, prettier, smarter, much more successful with boys, and more talented in the arts than I—*all at the same time,* to add insult to injury.

During most of high school, I wanted to be pretty enough to vie with these lovely young girls around me—though I didn't usually perceive myself to be attractive. Knowing that I was far from the most beautiful girl at school sometimes brought me to tears and confirmed that I would never have a boyfriend, or later, a husband. I regret to admit that at times I had envious fantasies about these girls suddenly losing 50 IQ points, or developing black eyes that would destroy their comeliness, or forfeiting their beautiful singing voices.

At the same time, I seriously believed that wearing makeup or styling my hair was nearly a "sin"—at least for me. For a short time during my sophomore year in high school, I clumsily experimented with lipstick, blush, mascara, and eye shadow to see what I was missing. But otherwise I prudishly kept my face severe, banishing the wish for "artificial" beautification. It wasn't until I was 26 or 27 that I first colored my hair, and even then did so with trepidation.

I can see now that my conviction that making up my face, or enhancing my appearance by wearing contact lenses, would show lack of character is repressive nonsense. Even so, today I rarely wear more makeup than lipstick, don glasses rather than contact lenses, and don't color my unruly, darkened hair. I tell myself my lack of beauty regimen is purely for convenience, but could it be that I've unconsciously still denied myself permission to look as attractive as I can? Maybe that's the reason I haven't been very successful with weight loss these past few years as well. I'm afraid to be noticed as an alluring person, so it's easier to make sure I remain ugly.

Perhaps it all points back to my fear of sex, first awakened by my initial attempt at self-injury back when I was eight years old. My anxiety over this awful mystery only built to a crescendo as I got older. In high school, it seemed to me that my sisters and friends were advertising themselves by wearing makeup and teasing their hair, to draw in the boys. The hypothesis seemed to fit according to my skewed "logic" because the girls who I "knew" by hearsay to be non-virgins also tended to pile on the makeup and even lighten their hair.

I told myself that I certainly didn't want to identify myself with "those" girls, or even let it be known that I was capable of being attracted to boys. Luckily for clueless me, my high school friends were "good girls" and hence didn't color their hair, wear much makeup, or drink at all—at least not around me.

In high school, I did act in school plays from time to time, however, even daring to talk, albeit bashfully, to boys from our "brother school." (I attended an all-girls parochial school.) And when I didn't win the roles I wanted in school plays and musicals, I sobbed for days with self-hatred and fear that I was no good. I took this kind of rejection so personally that I know now that even if I'd had sufficient acting talent (and luck) to make it in Hollywood or New York, I'd never have survived the rejections and setbacks that precede success.

I perhaps displayed a modicum of talent in the performing arts, but I don't delude myself anymore that I had the kind of incandescent presence required to be a Hollywood star. Back then, though, when I thought about colleges it was with an eye toward which ones had stellar drama departments. My dream of performing professionally ended once I made my entrance at Georgetown University, only to more than meet my match in the superior vocalists and actors among the student body. I couldn't even get a solo in the small church choir I belonged to, let alone a leading role in a student-run show. Perhaps this paved the way for my 180 degree turn to major in psychology instead, a much more sensible decision. But before arriving at that crossroads, I had to descend still further into a leaden, depressive fog.

MY FIRST EPISODE

As I entered my senior year of high school in 1984, I began agonizing over more serious matters than how my attractiveness or artistic talents compared with those of my sisters and classmates. I found myself more and more convinced that I was going to die soon. I just had an incontrovertible intuition that I was not long for this world. At that early point I did not yet contemplate suicide; my sense that God fumed at me and hence would arrange for a brutal death simply developed into an ever greater certainty.

And then, abruptly and paradoxically, I was at once dreading my death and plunging myself however haphazardly into life. It suddenly was urgent for me to design and conduct surveys among my classmates and teachers on handedness and creativity. To cut up and stitch patches on my Catholic girls' high school uniform in the middle of the night for no reason. To attend 6 a.m. Mass at the nearby convent every morning, after staying up most of the night attempting vainly to read ancient Greek history (in Greek, no less!) while drinking cold black coffee sprinkled with salt and pepper. Then, before daybreak, to wander in a daze down the street in my ratty nylon nightgown for a few blocks.

I revved on more cylinders than I previously knew I had. Buzzing energy suffused my brain and body, zapping me like lightning bolts that electrified me with a curious mixture of desperation and elation. At the time I felt effortlessly able to maintain my 4.0 average at my college-preparatory high school, as well as to work for 25 hours after classes at a specialty retail shop in the downtown area of Alexandria known as Old Town. I poured my effervescent heart into fashioning creative, colorful displays for merchandise, and I flitted around the shop restocking goods, chattily ringing up customers, and swinging a vacuum over the rugs when the store closed.

For a brief, brilliant period of time, life sparkled and spun around me. Every event and sensory experience, no matter how trivial, seemed imbued with special meaning just for me. If a school friend happened to be wearing the same color blouse as I on a certain day, I was sure this meant the two of us were mystically connected. Songs I heard on the radio seemed to hold special messages for me as well, telling of a perfect love that would soon be mine if only I was holy enough.

I even marveled at the jeweled hues of traffic lights at night. A green signal spotlighted against a dark blue sky seemed akin to van Gogh's masterpiece *The Starry Night*. Yellow traffic lights glistened like miniature moons, and red signals were ruddy coals. I danced dizzily through the hours on a gyroscope, watching impressionistic clouds fluffy with "ideas of reference"—convictions that every minor coincidence and communication I encountered was meant particularly for me, that every comment I heard on a bus or in a hall referred to me alone.

My bizarre behavior and agitation proved too intense to sustain, however. Within a few months my hyperactivity subsided, as an all-encompassing lethargy leeched through my pores. This near-stupor left me less and less able to maintain the demanding schedule of attaining my usual straight-As at school, keeping up my work schedule at the store in Old Town, and generally acting strange.

A final stumbling block felled me when post-secondary education loomed. I was supposed to be preparing for this crucial decision by researching, visiting, and applying to selective colleges and universities. While my parents puzzled over my inertness, I simply did nothing to secure a spot at any college whatsoever. I was completely incapable of even picking up a university brochure and writing away for a catalog, let alone arranging a visit to a campus, asking a teacher for a recommendation, or crafting an essay for an application. My senior year should have been one of the most exciting times of my life as I readied myself for the luminous four years ahead. Instead I sank deeper and deeper into a mire of sloth and despair.

Those straight As became Bs, then Cs and Ds, and I couldn't even make myself care. I began to detach myself from the world more and more, to ponder death again, but this time not as something God was planning for me, but as something that I could plan for myself as the only way out from the palpable shadow that had descended on and clung mercilessly to my shoulders. Formerly banal household objects like scissors and vegetable knives took on the sinister promise of ending my melancholy and thick-headed confusion.

I took to climbing out on the second-floor roof outside my bedroom late at night and talking woefully to myself, all the while wondering exactly how much damage I might do to myself if I jumped. Only my base cowardice kept me from acting on any of these impulses—until I became sicker still and started secretly punching holes in my wrist with pins and paper clips. Of course I didn't cause myself any serious injury, but told myself I was practicing for the time when the pain became so excruciating that I would finally have to act.

By now I had stopped attending high school and spent my days doing nothing but slouching in a chair in the living room watched by my family, my nights lying sleepless in bed with terrifying psychotic and suicidal ruminations circling around and around in my head without end. My family members had all but exhausted their emotional resources in caring for me. My closest-in-age sister, "Ellen," to whom I compared myself endlessly, couldn't understand why I was acting so weirdly unless it was to get attention in some sick way. I know I embarrassed her at school, while I was still attending, with my markedly odd, asocial behavior, and now I'm sorry she had to put up with that, with me. Of course, at the time I was oblivious to any effect I might have had on other people, blind to anything except the destructive whirlpool my moods had sucked me into.

And one of my most vivid memories of those days is the weekend afternoon while I was still going to school, when my parents lectured me about not having done a single thing toward getting into a single college, with deadlines fast approaching. "Are you on drugs?!" my dad asked in bafflement. My response to this was telling: I immediately broke down in a flood of tears, completely ashamed that my own parents could think I would ever take drugs. I must be more evil even than I had thought. This may have been the wake-up call they needed to realize I seriously needed help; it's not natural for an adolescent, however broody, to cry in response to a question that might instead elicit indignation or casuistic denial.

If my mom and dad didn't read the neon signs then, they had no choice but to accept that I was no longer their golden girl a few weeks later. It was a blustery, rainy November morning and I trudged the few blocks to school as usual—only to experience a sudden but utterly crushing panic after reaching my homeroom. All at once I gasped for breath, trembled convulsively, and my heart palpitated insistently. I felt suspended in air, as though floating outside myself. I knew I would die any moment, and my perceptual field collapsed to a singular, imperative need to ESCAPE! As the first class bell rang, I rushed out of the building without thinking and half-ran, half-walked down the meandering streets of our neighborhood.

By sheer luck I found myself at a bus stop. A city-bound bus soon appeared, which I boarded (I can't remember if I was even organized enough to pay the fare—I doubt it). On a whim I decided that once the bus stopped at a subway station, I would ride the subway to the college dormitory of an older acquaintance on whom I had a rather delusional crush. The fact that I didn't have any idea of his address other than the city—and that he certainly had never invited me to visit him—didn't figure into my chaotically unbalanced equation at all.

I was so far removed from reality that indeed I took the subway to what I hoped was the correct stop, in a state of physical panic the entire time. Then I emerged from the station and paced up and down unfamiliar streets in the pounding rain with no umbrella and no more money, until I reached an apartment building. Obviously I was unable to locate my friend (I had not even found the college), but I needed shelter, so with some sort of psychotic anti-logic I reasoned that if I hung around the apartment vestibule, I could gain several hours to calm down and consider either how to run away permanently from my intolerable life or gain the means and the guts to kill myself.

My nebulous "plans" were brought up short when after about half an hour the apartment manager, a brusque but well-meaning woman, descended the elevator to the lobby and discovered her disheveled, confused, and terrified "tenant." She probed repeatedly to elicit information—about my identity, my home address and parents' names and phone numbers—and tried to pry from me why and how I had ended up alone in her building in a rather seedy part of the city. For about an hour I was too paranoid and too incoherent to respond to her, but I finally caved and whispered to her the bare facts. Immediately afterward the apartment manager called first my parents to reassure them I was safe, and then the police, who had apparently been searching for me (alerted no doubt by my family). I know I was barely connected to reality at the time, but I do remember her commenting to the police in an undertone, "She's obviously emotionally disturbed." Well, that was an understatement.

All too soon my parents arrived and brought me home, nearly weeping in their relief at finding me and the revelation of how fragile I had become. I, however, had long since passed the point of being able to cry and silently fumed that I had not been allowed to escape from the life that was suffocating me. During an emotion-fraught discussion of the incident afterwards, I was unable to explain what had possessed me to flee from school and home so suddenly. In fact, I was unable to say much of anything to my parents. Shortly thereafter, they took me out of school, as I could no longer function there. After a couple of increasingly desperate weeks (on everyone's part) of round-the-clock monitoring, which proved insufficient to stop me from furtively trying to act on my suicidal impulses, my parents brought me to a local psychiatric hospital.

Before they reached this decision, I seem to remember my parents engaging repeatedly in scary, shouting arguments about whether I truly needed to be in a hospital. In my memory of their disagreements, my mother insisted that the family was doing fine watching me continuously, and feared the stigma I would face having a psychiatric hospitalization on my permanent record when I did apply to colleges. My father, on the other hand, didn't feel they could sufficiently protect me from my self-destructive impulses and thought a hospital was the safest place for me. But once they discovered the pinpricks dotting my wrists, they felt they had no other choice.

Much later, when I recounted my memory of the frightening, intense fights they had had on my behalf, my mother looked at me in surprise. "We never fought over that," she told me. "We were united in the idea that you needed to be hospitalized." So it seems that psychosis may once again have colored the way I perceived events around me.

At any rate, I secretly agreed with their decision; for some reason I welcomed being put in the hospital. On some level, the healthy part of me knew I needed to be in a completely safe place where I could be treated intensively with medications and therapy. I also still wanted an escape from the daily life that had become unbearable to me, and I thought the hospital would provide it. In the hospital I wouldn't have to worry about the schoolwork I was missing, the colleges I hadn't applied to, the concerned family I experienced as intrusive. That I would still have to contend with my delusions of being evil, my urges to hurt myself, and of course the overpowering gloom that seemed to have taken up permanent residence in my being, didn't occur to me.

IN THE HOSPITAL

Twenty-six years later, I can still easily summon the memory of that awful first night in the psychiatric hospital in November 1984. A pleasant but impersonal nurse conducted an interview—to me, an interrogation—about my immediate past and current psychiatric symptoms, probing with especial detail into my suicidal ideation and actions. Upon determining that I was indeed a suicide risk, she set up a mattress and blanket on the floor of the "quiet room" and told me to get some sleep, and that the doctor would be there in the morning. It was the day after Thanksgiving, but I didn't feel I had anything in particular to give thanks for. I hadn't escaped my private hell after all.

As had been my wont for a couple of months by that time, I slept barely at all that night. Instead, I ruminated, negative-feedback-looped, about my evilness and listened, wide-eyed, to the occasional yells of the other patients on this adolescent ward. I was to discover that teenagers with all sorts of diagnoses had been lumped in together on this unit: young people with drug and alcohol problems and "acting out" behaviors (whom I referred to in my prejudiced mind as "juvenile delinquents"); pregnant girls whose families had given up on them; and other kids like me with depression, mania, and/or florid psychosis all shared this crowded corridor.

The other patients, particularly the louder ones and especially the boys (remember, I had gone to an all-girls school) frightened me into a curled-inward knot of silence in the first few days of what would be a month-long stay. For days I dared not speak, and when I finally did, I hung my head low and could not make eye contact with anyone, staff or peer.

But back to the first morning after my all-night vigil: I was ordered up by another nurse and commanded to take a shower. At this, my fuzzy mind churned with bewilderment and anxiety: I knew I hadn't been able to shower or bathe in at least a week and had no inclination to do so now. On the other hand, if I didn't obey these authority figures, who knew what would happen? In the end, I haphazardly unpacked my belongings in the room I'd share with two other girls and clung to the bed awaiting an inspiration to penetrate the fog of my mind.

Then an inspiration did come. Since I seemed to have been left blessedly alone for a few minutes, I proceeded to bang my head as forcefully but as quietly as I could manage against the bedroom wall. To my astonishment, I was not discovered and began to think that maybe I wouldn't be as safe here as had been hoped. Maybe later I'd even get a chance to go at my wrist with another safety pin. This, alas, was not to be. Staff members soon examined me, discovered my puncture marks and knew what to watch out for.

In between encountering frightening teenagers and negotiating group therapy, where I was forced to actually speak and give my name and the reason I was here, I met with my new psychiatrist, a man who looked astonishingly like the college boy I'd tried vainly to visit the day I'd shot out of high school in a panic. *This must be a sign,* I told myself—*the object of my crush has somehow been transformed into this doctor who will solve all my problems.* My hopes were dashed over the next few weeks, however, as I came to discover that this "magical" psychiatrist had no patience for my earnest recitation of my psychotic symptoms, dismissing my delusions and ruminations and telling me brusquely "not to think about that."

As the month between Thanksgiving and Christmas progressed, I found myself assimilating into the adolescent ward culture despite my hesitation. True, I never felt comfortable around my psychiatrist, and the teacher at the "school" program we were required to attend seemed somewhat tyrannical. Once he assigned us to write poetry, an instruction with which I eagerly complied. As I scribbled my idiosyncratic verse, he ordered us each to read our poems aloud. I begged off, saying my verse was too personal to share. The teacher simply restated his command, so I balled up my piece of paper and put it in my mouth and chewed it, in a pathetic attempt at rebellion. Somehow this teacher got me to spit out my poem, then read it (what was still legible after being in my mouth) to himself, commenting only, "You're weird." At least I was spared having to recite the poem, but I felt humiliated.

A SUICIDAL CRISIS
AND ITS RESOLUTION

I did experience one major setback toward the end of my hospitalization. I should mention that my devoted family visited me *every single day* during my stay. My mother and father would come to the clamorous dayroom, always accompanied by at least one or two of my many brothers and sisters. Following the natural course of a mood disorder, I had been at that point feeling particularly dejected for the past week when my parents and my then-10-year-old sister visited one evening.

Some of my spirit had returned as the medicines had begun to work despite the lingering depression by that time. So on this particular evening, I blurted to my father in willful desperation that if I had to leave the hospital at the end of the month, "I really will kill myself." At this point accustomed to my mood swings, he handled this threat calmly enough, but my little sister became upset and tried to comfort me. With an irritable edge, I ordered her to "Shut up!" and she burst into tears. I'm still ashamed of my conduct—she must have been so scared for me, and then I dumped my pain on her. And who at 10 can handle having a suicidal sister?

The next afternoon I managed to steal some time to myself while holed up in my bedroom and grabbed a pencil to start on some "homework." Still angry and agitated, I suddenly realized the full potential of that pencil. Despite my having begun to recover, I had regained just enough energy to carry out my destructive wishes, and I was fully as suicidal as I had been immediately prior to entering the hospital. Impulsively I snapped the pencil in half, seized one of the jagged pieces, and scraped at my wrist. I continued to dig into my wrist with the pencil scrap, but just as I began to draw blood, my roommate entered the bedroom. Instantly understanding, she grabbed the pencil out of my hand and yelled for staff. They hurried in, confiscated the pencil, bandaged my wrist, and deposited me in the quiet room. My next dose of antidepressant was stronger than the previous ones.

Though frustrated then in having been thwarted in my mission to end my dysphoria, I now feel divinely lucky that I was rescued from my suicide attempt. After that I somehow learned how to mingle comfortably with most of my fellow patients, even some of the loud boys. Emerging from my depression with the help of psychotherapy, my family's love and support, and a drug cocktail of antidepressants, antipsychotics, and lithium certainly helped in this effort, as did my inborn eagerness to please and docile personality. In time, I lifted my head from the floor, spoke to people, and even learned to smile and laugh again as my depression and psychosis lifted. I even developed the requisite hospital crush, on one of my fellow patients.

As mentioned, my family's steadfast love and the healing I experienced through my art therapy and writing hastened recovery, and I left the hospital on the day before Christmas, just as my insurance ran out. It was truly the happiest Christmas of my life. I had skidded to the brink of death and been blessed to return to life.

My parents, school teachers and administrators, and I mutually agreed that I would take off the rest of the school year and retake my senior year the following autumn. This decision greatly relieved the pressure of making up the mountains of schoolwork I had feared I would face. On the other hand, I was left with lots of spare time to fill during days when I would normally have been attending high school. At the time (late 1984 and early 1985), no day program or clinic filled with therapeutic activities and groups existed for me to attend.

With my family, I cobbled together a makeshift solution to this dilemma that involved my going to work with alternately my mother or father, where I would read or collate papers for mailings. Later I was able to find part-time work at a local after-school daycare program, a consignment shop, and a McDonald's. I was able to cope fairly well with these jobs, except for the one at McDonald's, where the frantic pace and long hours on my feet exhausted and nerve wracked me. After three weeks of increasing stress, I summoned the courage (though it felt like cowardice at the time) to tell my managers I was quitting—and was assertive enough to resist pressure from them to continue working there.

At the same time I continued to see a psychiatrist and psychologist for medication management and interpersonal therapy, respectively. My outpatient psychiatrist was a gentle, fatherly man who took seriously my symptoms and recitations of how I was coping, instead of dismissing them as adolescent drama (as I felt my doctor in the hospital had done).

My mother and father had chosen from among the very best experts in adolescent psychiatry and mood disorders, and they had chosen well; I truly trusted this doctor and was able to describe my experiences to him, knowing he could help me. Although he is no longer my psychiatrist, having moved on to academic distinction across the country, I send to and receive from him a holiday card every year to this day.

I also was able to find solace and understanding in my psychotherapist, a woman about my mother's age with young daughters of her own. She sprinkled her practical advice about handling the academic, job, and interpersonal stresses of adolescence with anecdotes from her own high school and college experiences. From her I received not only skillful parsing of my particular challenges but warm nurturance and spiritual guidance, during the three years—my two senior years and the first year of college—that I saw her. Years later I was shocked and profoundly saddened to hear that this seminal figure from my young adulthood had given her life aboard United Airlines Flight 93 on September 11, 2001. What a tremendous loss for her family and all her young patients—she touched the lives of so many with her sensible caring and clinical skills.

MY SECOND SENIOR YEAR

While continuing to see these specialists, I entered my "second senior year" in the fall of 1985 with eagerness tempered with apprehension. I would be attending classes with a whole different set of girls from my previous (graduated) class. Doubtless these young women would know, as would my teachers, what had happened to me. What kind of welcome would I receive, I wondered? Would I be stared at, whispered about, patronized, snubbed?

I needn't have worried—for the most part my peers and teachers treated me with the same warmth as they always had, at least to my face. I soon assembled a group of friends to eat lunch with and visit on weekends and after school. And I convinced my teachers I could handle the schoolwork with the same diligence I had always exhibited, save for during my erstwhile depression. In fact, I flourished that second senior year, succeeding (for once) beyond even my expectations. Once again, I made straight As; I earned SAT scores of 700+ on each subtest. I (finally!) applied to four colleges and secured acceptance at all four, choosing Georgetown University, which awarded me scholarship money as well as loans.

I played the lead in our spring musical comedy, "Bells Are Ringing," and thoroughly enjoyed doing so, cherishing the experiences I felt a "normal" teenager should have as much as the memories they created. I also attended the senior prom with a male friend I'd met during rehearsals and performances of the musical—something I never would have predicted could happen to ugly, antisocial me. I graduated in May 1986 as salutatorian of my class, with my mood-disordered past behind me—or so my family and I believed.

In the early days after I emerged from my initial psychotic depression in high school, my parents and I convinced ourselves that it would be my only episode, that I would enjoy perfect mental health from then on. And who could blame us for wanting to avoid the messiness, angst, and deflected pursuit of normal life goals that both my family and I had endured? But alas, that was wishful thinking. One of the most striking features of mood

36

disorders is their recurrent nature. Over and over again, I've heard the same hope from other consumers with all types of mental illnesses, and from their family members as well: *This will be the only time this devastating event dares to happen to me, to us.* Unfortunately, I've noticed (and so have many others, both laypeople and scientists) that these illnesses tend to evolve and revolve over time. Those of us who have serious depression, bipolar disorder, or schizophrenia, in particular, tend to experience more complicated or treatment-resistant episodes in greater numbers as time passes.

GEORGETOWN: BLUE AND GRAY

Looking back, that's certainly been true for me, as I recall the turmoil of my college days. As I have recounted, my initial depression was immediately preceded by what appeared to be a series of simple panic attacks; they evolved into a brief hypomania/agitated depression, which then stretched into a stuporous, psychotic depression leading to my hospitalization.

At Georgetown, more hypomanias and then manias emerged, as I developed full-blown bipolar disorder. During those same years, as I reached my early 20s, I began to experience a different type of psychosis with paranoid ideation—even being diagnosed by one doctor as having schizoaffective disorder, bipolar type. I doubt this is the correct diagnosis for me, as all the other psychiatrists I've consulted have labeled me bipolar, but it is true that from time to time I've worried about people talking about me, a fear that began during college.

Perhaps precipitated by the tricyclic antidepressants I continue to take but first took in 1984, I also began to experience rapid cycling of hypomania and depression after a couple of years at college. Since then, I've been prone from time to time to ultradian mood cycles, during which I swing from a cheerful or irritable hypomania to sluggish, tear-stained depression in the span of a week. On a few occasions, my moods have cycled significantly even within a single day.

And the anxiety that was the first harbinger of my psychiatric problems never fully left me. In college, I worried irrationally and incessantly about every little thing possible, especially the schoolwork that I couldn't always complete, to the point that it sometimes prevented me from sleeping. And unlike most of my university peers, I could not (and still cannot) drive a car, thanks to my unreasonable phobia of accidentally causing or being the victim of an auto accident. It was also during my time at Georgetown that I began to startle disproportionately at sudden noises, even jumping out of my seat at an unexpected sound.

My Georgetown saga, as I melodramatically thought of it, was a raucous college collage of barely contained emotions; both exceptional and failing grades; so-called relationships that really weren't and friendships I didn't know how to have; cramming study sessions; three-in-the-morning burning conversations; and self-injury that served as the bleak backdrop of my story then.

Luckily for me, my college years did not involve drugs or, save for as many drinks as I could count on one hand in all four years, alcohol—since I knew on an elemental level not to mess with my brain any further than it had already been interfered with by illness.

The hodge-podge that composed those years can best be summarized by excerpts from a journal I kept during my senior year, from 1989 to 1990. The front inside cover of the journal, which a friend had given me, features a marvelous (as I now see it) quote from Joan Baez:

"You are amazing grace. You are a precious jewel. You—special, miraculous, unrepeatable, fragile, fearful, tender, lost, sparkling ruby emerald jewel rainbow splendor person."

In the lower left-hand corner of the paper bearing the quote, I had written, in a small, cramped hand, "yeah, right."

*   *   *   *

"Sunday, December 10, 1989:

"Tremor: a little. I don't think it's being a big problem. Localized in the hands, every once in a while spreads to the arms. I'll just have to see whether it worsens.

"Sleep: it had been going all over the place! But the cycle seems to have shifted in the past few days from getting by on a few hours a night with no naps or even staying up all night, to sleeping 9 or 10 hours a night and feeling more lethargic. It could be associated with switching into a depression, for which there is a little evidence. Let me see if I can work backwards . . . Last night I went to bed at 2 a.m. and woke up at 12:30 p.m. feeling as if I could have even slept more. Friday night I stayed up talking to friends in the dorm and went to bed at 4 or 4:30 a.m. Woke up at 9:30 a.m. for the DC Schools Project [a tutoring program for high school students learning English as a second language that I was involved in as part of my special dorm floor], but then took a nap in the afternoon from 3 to 6 p.m."

*   *   *   *

"Friday, December 15, 1989:

"I know my mood has something, if not a lot, to do with my sleep patterns. Which causes which, or if it's causal at all, I'm not sure—but when I was averaging four or five hours a night, including two nights of not sleeping at all, I was hypomanic. When I started sleeping more, I got a little depressed. Or vice versa. I remember going through Wednesday on no sleep at all the night before, getting at least seven hours that night (well, really Thursday morning), and waking up slightly depressed. I slept 10½ hours last night, still feel sleepy, and am definitely tending toward the depressed side of the spectrum. Though my mood still shifts sometimes."

"I've been more depressed these past few days, what with worrying about how I'm doing in my classes. But good things happening unexpectedly, like getting an A on a test, have an uplifting temporary effect on me (reactive, that's called). I've had a little bit of just lying on the bed thinking in circles or napping. Often prefer to be alone in the dining hall, but at other times am normally sociable. A few instances of painful nostalgia and feeling jealous of or incompetent beside another person. It's a tiny bit dark."

"I think my moods have been flip-flopping back and forth to an extent; sometimes they switch almost instantaneously, and I can't tell what the hell is going on. Sometimes I just want to explode my head to get all the toxic waste out!"

"Had a sudden thought—that I immediately recognized as irrational—that Y was plotting to kill me. There's still some tension between us, because Y doesn't know I am suspicious of her, but I still think she talks about me all the time. Even though I guess the thought was unrealistic, it still bothered me."

"The next day, I heard that a friend of mine had a grandmother die. I really wanted to hug her and say, 'I hope you feel better,' or, 'Let me know if there's anything I can do,' but I felt so awkward and uncomfortable. I was also ashamed of myself because, when my Grandma died, I didn't cry. I never cried, not even to this day—I don't understand it, how can a depressive not cry?! I guess I was sort of numb, maybe from all these medications."

"Exams—procrastinating studying. Feel guilty for not studying as much or having as many exams as some of the others. Thoughts a little disorganized, but I think today's exam went well anyway. After it was over, I did get a little upset ruminating about how I'd done. So I cut my thigh, hip, and a little bit on my wrist with a razor this evening. Then I was a little dazed, and then I put "normalcy" back on so I could go eat dinner at the cafeteria."

"I'm taking incompletes for a couple of classes, and now that exams are over I'm supposed to be working on writing papers for these classes. I haven't worked on the papers yet. I guess I'll have to do it all at home. I have a definite block about them right now. I've been reading a little but haven't taken any notes though. I haven't been able, or willing, to write anything. It's probably not depression, just my laziness and lack of motivation that makes it so hard. Sometimes I hate myself for my sloth. Last night I banged my head on the wall when my roommate was out because I put out my books in front of me with my notebooks and pen, and then I felt completely overwhelmed and just started crying. It seemed like only the head-banging would help. It did help in the immediate present, but the whole next day I had a ringing headache."

* * * *

[This next excerpt concerns a composite character, a boy representing the several young men I wished to date during the college years, whom I've identified only by a falsified initial, and my reactions to a hoped-for relationship that did not work out.]

"Someone who's been on my mind—too much—is X. I feel incredibly attracted to him, but that's not a good idea because he seems like the type who will charm you but never commit. I already have to do all the work just to keep our 'friendship' (or whatever this weird relationship is) going. I knock on his door; I leave notes and candy-canes and apologize all the time. All of which leads me to believe that X doesn't really like me romantically anyway. And then I invited X to come over to our dorm floor and see our Christmas tree, which has all these ornaments I designed and made myself. In fact, I cut out and painted ornaments when I should have been studying, you might say. Still, I waited until 2 a.m. and X never showed up.

"So then I went into the vestibule of the dorm, where I could sort of hide out, and cried a little and banged my head repeatedly. The first time I'd hurt myself in about a month, I think. I couldn't think of any other way to express things, though. All I've done with my sense of fury and powerlessness is to use violence against myself."

"So I cried and banged my head and thought how I'm not good enough for anyone. So far I haven't been good enough for anyone I've ever liked or loved. Am I ever going to be good enough for anyone to love me—someone

I also love? Do I have any right to seek out a boyfriend—and later a husband—when I'm disabled? Would anyone want me? It's my monstrous pride, but it's also loneliness and feeling there's something fundamentally *wrong* with me—like I'm the one unmatchable sock in the universe. Is it my 'condition'?"

"You shouldn't put your hopes on anyone or anything. You just should never expect that anything good is going to happen, because it won't. You shouldn't think anyone cares, because they don't. This is why I'm having suicidal thoughts—flashes of taking all my pills at once or jumping off the highest building on campus, or cutting my wrists deeply. I don't think I'm really going to do it. I just get impulses when I think about how no one gives a damn, and why should they, when I'm sickened by the thought of myself. I need nurturance from other people, but I can't ask for it when I've no right to it."

"Where do the condemning voices (well, thoughts, not hallucinations) at the back of my head come from? Well, I say to myself, 'you're not good enough,' 'you're ugly,' 'stand up straight,' 'you're fat,' 'you're not as smart or pretty as so-and-so,' 'I made a fool out of myself,' 'you're too shy and you should open up more,' 'you're screwing up,' 'WHAT IS THE MATTER WITH YOU?' "

"I'm getting scared. Last night I went out to the courtyard where no one ever goes and talked to myself for an hour or so—then I cut myself slightly with a scissors blade on the wrist, though it wasn't a suicide attempt. There is diurnal variation, but this feels more like a settling-down global condition, a flattening and glooming instead of an acute episode. This is starting to feel like it did when it all started five and one-half years ago. That's what I mean by the DSM-III-R's 'distinct quality of mood.' Am not talking to people unless I have to. I'm getting sedated and sleeping through my alarm, hence through classes, again. I don't feel like doing anything. Behind on papers. Takes me too long to write them. Neglecting hygiene—taking shower, brushing teeth, washing face. Self-disgust. I feel like I'm not all here—I just don't care."

"Another feeling I've been experiencing lately is wanting people to acknowledge the hard times I've gone through and still go through—though this is motivated by totally selfish instincts. But still, you don't get college credit for depression and hypomania and instability. No one sees that, or if they do, they don't acknowledge it. No one notices any more that I struggle. And no one else really knows the hell I descend into every time I get depressed; there's no way they can. So I'm supposed to act like the depression doesn't exist, I guess, but I can never stop remembering that it does. I live with it all the time, every time I take a pill, even when I'm not in an episode."

"The reason I'm afraid of not being depressed, of being taken for normal, expected to perform as normal, is I'm afraid of what's going to happen when people see I'm not perfect, I'm not going to always be what they want, and I see as well that I'm not always going to be what people want. And I've always depended on other people for my definition of who I am, who I should be, and for my self-esteem. So, what am I if you take all of them away? Do I exist at all? Maybe it's easier to kill yourself if you've never had an identity to begin with—if there's really nothing there to destroy in the first place."

*   *   *   *

Of course, I did not kill myself while I was at Georgetown, and needless to say, I was followed by both an excellent psychiatrist and empathic psychotherapist to whom I could confide my academic concerns, fears, and broken hearts. My self-injury was for the most part para-suicidal rather than outright suicidal, and since it served the purpose of an emotional outlet, however unhealthy, it didn't usually occur to me then, in my late teens and early 20s, that better outlets existed.

On the other hand, from time to time I resonated with my inner muse and created colorful, emotionally raw abstract paintings or wrote tortuous poems about my journey through the jungle of bipolar disorder. Prone at times to grandiosity, I saw these artistic creations as much more skillfully rendered than they probably were. But I have no way of knowing the quality of my art and poetry now; all my creations were given away back then with the pompous certainty that their recipients would doubtless treasure them.

As well, the dark days of hiding out and hurting myself were balanced by carefree days of spirited philosophical discussions that lasted for hours, learning madrigals in the choir, enjoying the company of the high school girl I tutored each week and her brother and sisters, as well as my many acquaintances (I could be quite outgoing when in the mood to be), and even, believe it or not, learning some wonderful things about psychology, my chosen major.

I secretly chuckled when an abnormal psychology professor mispronounced the name of the very antidepressant I was taking along with lithium and Depakote. And secretly fumed when another teacher in a biology class opined that conditions like heart disease required constant proactivity to control, "Unlike bipolar disorder, where if you just take your lithium, you're fine." No, that's not all it takes, I felt like answering, but did not, wishing to keep my identity as a "bipolar person" (as I thought of myself then) under cover.

When the cause was close to my heart, I could be an activist, though. In October of my junior year, I organized a campus forum during Mental Illness Awareness Week, on Depression Awareness Day. Maybe I was ahead of my time, since this (in 1989) was well before the modern-day widespread campus presence of students allied with campus mental health professionals to support students with depression.

I single-handedly printed up posters to advertise the forum. One design read, "Abraham Lincoln had clinical depression. But they didn't call him crazy. They called him Mr. President," and another design listed famous people who had mood disorders, such as Winston Churchill and Virginia Woolf. Fueled by hypomania, I ran around campus taping up posters and talking up the event, for which I'd assembled such speakers as a psychiatrist and a relative, who was an executive at NAMI (National Alliance on Mental Illness).

On the day of the event, I introduced the speakers and watched the auditorium with drawn breath to gauge the other students' interest. More than 80 kids attended—not bad, considering there was also a home basketball game that evening. And I was told, without breaking confidentiality, that several students had since visited Student Health to be screened for mood disorders. More even than a perfect 100 grade, I felt this to be my finest moment at college—I was fulfilling my barely-conceived calling even before I could become a mental health professional.

POST-COLLEGE:
BEFORE THE SECOND STORM

In my four years at Georgetown, I had garnered some lasting friends, five of whom I had arranged to live with in a townhouse close to the campus, which we rented in the fall after graduation. Living away from home on a more-or-less permanent basis, working full-time, and paying my own rent gave me my first taste of Adult Life.

True, I frequently came back home over the weekends, and I still tutored my ESOL student, who was now preparing to graduate from high school, every Saturday. I also sang in an alt-rock band that I had formed with a few Georgetown students who had yet to graduate, often socializing with these friends on weekends when I wasn't visiting my family. But I did seem to be handling life after graduation fairly well once I settled into the routine of a steady job and a regular social schedule.

During the summers between college academic years, I had worked on the adult schizophrenia research unit at NIMH (the National Institute of Mental Health). While there I had sponged up state-of-the-art information about schizophrenia and mental illness in general, eagerly attending rounds, assisting with research procedures, spinning blood samples in centrifuges, and keying research data into the NIMH computer system. My work there, although comprised of low-level duties deemed appropriate for a college student, served to confirm my calling—as I truly felt it to be—to work in the mental health field on behalf of people like me who lived with serious mental illnesses.

By September 1990, several months after graduation, I had managed to secure an entry-level full-time job as a research assistant on the same schizophrenia research unit at NIMH. I gratefully returned to work there, and this time began learning how to administer neuropsychological test batteries to research subjects, both healthy controls and inpatients or outpatients with schizophrenia.

That first November out of college, I was still struggling to make up the coursework and assignments for an incomplete grade I had received in developmental psychology. Though I'd taken three summer classes at Northern Virginia Community College to compensate for electives I'd withdrawn from, this incomplete still hung over my head. There was no escaping it—I'd been a psychology major, so letting the work go was not an option. And I wouldn't be considered to have officially graduated until I finished the final paper. Yet I buried my head in the sand and pretended the problem didn't exist.

Until the day an ominous-looking letter arrived from the Georgetown Department of Psychology. I pretty much knew what that letter contained: a mandate for me to either finish the work or not graduate—but I was too scared to open it just the same.

Another factor complicated this situation as well: I'd gone without one of my most important prescriptions—Depakote, my mood stabilizer—for about five days. This was due chiefly to my lack of communication with my parents, not a wish to be noncompliant. While I was living in the shared townhouse, I had very little money until I found the position at NIMH, and not much to live on even after that. Accordingly, my parents generously paid for my meds, obtaining my prescriptions for me and giving them to me on weekends. Because I didn't have my Depakote, my mood state was labile and I felt quite vulnerable.

So, as I sat trembling with the unopened letter on my lap, my anxiety grew exponentially as the seconds ticked by. Before I knew it, my terror had escalated into a florid manic/panic state. The fit struck with the full force of my high school anxiety attack from five years prior. Once again, I couldn't breathe; I felt as though I were going to die imminently; I chattered incessantly and incoherently about my terror; and I began pacing in tighter and tighter circles. I felt completely out of control, and I must have appeared so as well—when I gasped to my friends, "I need to go to the emergency room," they dropped everything and drove me double-time the (fortunately) few blocks to the Georgetown University Hospital ER.

Once in the ER, I catapulted myself back and forth within the tense, close waiting area, chanting "I'm going to die I'm going to die!" When escorted into a curtained room to wait for the psychiatrist, I rocked and rocked compulsively back and forth, growing more agitated by the second. A nurse informed me that staff were calling my parents; I cried, "No! They're going to hurt me! They'll hurt me!" which became my new mantra. Then I began singing tunelessly to "Edelweiss" from *The Sound of Music*; I couldn't have said why. I clutched at the flower designs painted onto the wall and shook my head as I sang and rocked. The nurse reentered the room to administer a mini-mental status exam or some similar questionnaire, but I was unable to answer most of the questions. I was driven too far internally to focus on what she was saying, and my attention was funneled now into the horror of what my parents would do to me when they arrived.

This last preoccupation bordered on delusional, since when my mom and dad did rush the 10 miles from Alexandria, VA, they expressed deep love and concern, without even a touch of anger or vindictiveness. They only wanted to help me, not hurt me. When it was time for the psychiatrist to interview me, somehow I snapped out of my storm to insist that my own doctor be summoned instead of this woman I had never seen before.

In fact my private psychiatrist did arrive on the scene, and was ready to hospitalize me on a psychiatric ward in a nearby hospital where he had admitting privileges. But the ER doctor had a quicker remedy: first she had an orderly shoot me with 1 or 2 mg of Ativan in the rear. Within 20 minutes I stopped rocking and singing myself into a frenzy and calmed down sufficiently to go home with my parents.

For the next two weeks, I lived at my family home instead of with my housemates in Georgetown, under the supervision of my parents and my psychiatrist. I immediately started back on my Depakote, taking an increased dose to ward off further mania. During those weeks, I did experience a few pacing fits along with self-destructive urges, telling my parents I had to cut my wrists to punish myself. Needless to say, my mom and dad prevented me from doing any damage to myself, and shortly thereafter the episode ran its course and I returned to the DC townhouse and to work at NIMH. This experience taught me two vital lessons:

1. Bipolar disorder can strike when you're not expecting it—you can't control that.
2. Go to therapy sessions, communicate with your family, and take your meds! You can control that.

SECOND STORM RISING

I should have known that the clearing of this last episode was actually the proverbial calm before a more violent storm. At the end of that academic year (spring 1991), the lease on our townhouse expired, and my friends and I dispersed. I ended up sharing another house in the Georgetown neighborhood with five girls, only one of whom was an acquaintance before I moved in. As the summer wore on, I noticed that I was having more and more trouble doing the daily chores I'd been assigned on the "duty wheel" that one of the young women had designed to ensure the smooth functioning of the household. In fact, waking up on time for work, socializing with friends and family, even getting out of bed on weekends was becoming ever more difficult. My intensifying depression was accompanied by a resurgence of urges to cut myself, and I began once again to contemplate suicide.

At the same time, my rapid mood cycling resumed, and I swung from sluggish depression to agitated, painful mania. I also found myself burdened again with psychotic symptoms: the absolute conviction that everyone at work; all my family members and friends; heck, anyone who even passed me on the street was talking about me and planning to humiliate me behind my back.

I also started to believe that people could read my mind, particularly people close to me such as family members, and especially my mom and dad. I would try to "shield" my thoughts from their scrutiny by imagining a steel wall around my brain, but it was usually no use—I somehow just "knew" that they could tell what I was thinking about them anyway. Though I was now prescribed antipsychotics again, such as Loxitane and Stelazine, these delusions grew quite frightening.

My conviction that I was unwillingly transmitting my thoughts to others around me despite the mental "shields" I erected occupied all of my attention—to the point that, one Monday during a rounds meeting at work, a wave of paranoia washed over me and I had to run out of the room to escape everyone there reading my thoughts. I was barely functioning during the days at NIMH by then, and often went so far as to sneak into restrooms on other floors and cut myself with scissors I'd grabbed from my desk and secreted in my lab coat pockets.

In the middle of that summer, I joined my family on a two-week vacation, driving across the country to visit friends in New Mexico. What should have been a deeply enriching experience enhanced by the sheer beauty and grandeur of the red, mountainous earth comprising the Santa Fe, Taos, and Albuquerque landscapes was instead little more than a forced march through various landmarks and a temporary respite from the black hole that I considered my everyday life back home to be.

My parents realized that I was depressed and not myself. As I prepared to return to Washington, DC, they "coached" me on polite remarks about my trip that I could offer to curious coworkers and housemates. They knew that I wouldn't have been able to summon such pleasantries through my own efforts.

After the New Mexico vacation, life settled down to bleakness as I had known it would. My suicidal ideation only worsened, and with the rest of my family still away across the country, I called on my beloved (now late) grandmother for help. She had undergone depression and psychosis herself as a young woman and understood much of what I was experiencing. She also lived nearby and invited me to stay with her until my family returned from their extended trip. The love she generously gave me—through listening carefully and responding gently to me—created a welcome recess from my anxiety, but didn't stop the root problem. I still felt sufficient angst to want to escape life permanently.

My intermittent dysphoric hypomanias also worsened. I began to engage in periodic, sudden fits of pacing in circles or up and down halls, unable to rein in my nervous energy, racing thoughts of self-destruction churning through my brain. On one occasion, my very gracious psychiatrist, certainly acting above and beyond the call of duty, walked with me around a Montgomery County (MD) shopping center parking lot as I paced furiously, until my parents could get there to pick me up.

Shortly after that incident, I moved straight from my grandmother's house back to my family home and away from the anxiety-ridden townhouse with its "duty wheel." My mom and dad could not help but perceive how desperate I had become, and with my psychiatrist's and my own agreement, they decided to take me back to the same psychiatric hospital where I had stayed in as an adolescent. This time, as I had reached the age of 23, I stayed on the adult ICU. I was admitted on "constant-watch" status, which meant that a female nurse or psych tech accompanied me even to the bathroom and to shower.

A new psychiatrist took over my case, a genuine, empathic man who took the time to meet with me every day while I was inpatient, and who quickly shook up my med regimen. To ameliorate my constant self-injurious, suicidal urges and paranoia, he substituted the (then) brand-new atypical antipsychotic Clozaril for my akathisia-producing Stelazine. He lowered my tremor-producing lithium and titrated my more tolerable and more effective Depakote upward. He also gave me Anafranil, a tricyclic antidepressant, to replace the hypomania-driving MAOI Nardil and to help me cope with the obsessive thoughts of self-destruction that crowded my mind.

Dramatic changes occurred within a week or two. I stopped wanting and trying to hurt myself to the exception of all else. I stopped believing that everyone around me was talking about me and reading my thoughts. My moods evened out, and the pacing storms were no more. My family and I were incredibly grateful to my new psychiatrist for helping me manage the acute illness so well, and we decided to ask him to take over my case on an outpatient basis, to which he agreed. After three weeks, I was released from the hospital in a vastly improved state. I was able to return to work at NIMH about a week later, astonished to discover that my colleagues were (surprise!) no longer plotting against me, that I could actually focus and concentrate on my duties, and that the office had overall become a much more pleasant place.

My new doctor met with me once a week for an hour, conducting both medication management and psychotherapy for some years to come. I found the combination tremendously healing and learned to grow back some of my lost self-esteem and to express some of my pent-up feelings—which I had previously expressed only against myself in the form of physical wounds. After a few months of emoting and theorizing in therapy with my psychiatrist, I finally ceased my lifelong habit of hurting myself. From late 1991 to this day (and my fingers are crossed for the future), I have never cut myself again, and I never plan to for the rest of my life. I credit my doctor with laying the foundation for this transformation, but he told me I must credit my own strength and determination as well. So I'll just say that he helped me rediscover the healthy part of myself, and since then I've helped her grow and mature.

In therapy I learned that being angry with someone, far from being an indicator of permanent hatred as I had believed as a child (and in fact up to that point as an adult), was simply a valid emotion that had a rightful place in close relationships of all kinds. When I (inevitably) felt it, I simply needed to find a way to properly express that anger. My doctor suggested, and I discovered, that I could actually talk about my anger with a friend, family member, or boyfriend instead of bottling it up and later cutting or burning myself or head-banging. This idea was revolutionary at first, particularly given my extreme lack of assertiveness. But my doctor and I practiced, over and over again, confronting people toward whom I had negative emotions: he would have me look at an empty chair and urge me to tell the "person" exactly what I wanted to say to her or him. Then he would give constructive feedback, which I used to amend and perfect my remarks before trying them out (usually successfully) in real life.

The only real downside to the newly healthy life I was now enjoying came in the form of side effects of Clozaril, my otherwise extraordinarily effective antipsychotic. I felt the very opposite of suicidal, yet I didn't feel completely alive because the drug was causing extreme sedation. I was quite often late or almost late for work in the morning, because rising from a drugged sleep proved a Herculean task. Once I did embark onto the subway train, I more often than not fell completely back asleep and missed my stop. I also found myself taking frequent involuntary "naps" while at the office or falling asleep during meetings, none of which was helping my productivity or the image of competence I wanted to project (especially considering that I'd just returned from a stay in a psychiatric hospital). And to add to the humiliation, I drooled prodigiously while I slept, even if only for a few minutes' nap.

But the worst side effect by far was the insidious weight gain that had begun almost the first day I took Clozaril. Although I was ingesting a relatively low dose, I gained more than 50 pounds within my first two years on the drug. I had always maintained a perfectly normal, if not model-slim, weight for my height in the past; now I was growing ever pudgier, or as I saw it in self-disgust, fat as a whale. I wasn't sure whether my appetite had increased, or whether my metabolism had simply slowed down, or maybe both in concert. In the end, what mattered to me was how much I hated the way I'd started to look and feel. My ever-mounting weight gain was slowing me down as much as the sedation.

I pleaded with my doctor to switch me to a drug that would not pile the weight on. In the summer of 1993, he invited me to participate in a trial pitting Clozaril against a (then) new antipsychotic, Risperdal, which purportedly did not cause the same degree of weight gain. I accepted the challenge and went through the double-blind study. Luckily, my course was fairly smooth. At the midpoint (during the cross-taper, when the dosage for one drug was lowered while the other was raised). I did experience moderate depression for a few weeks, but it wasn't nearly as severe as the episodes I'd undergone before both hospitalizations.

As was revealed to me after the trial ended, I had first been on Clozaril for some weeks, then had a cross-taper period, then had taken Risperdal for a few weeks more. The study clinicians' weekly behavioral ratings and weekly weight records demonstrated, in my case at least, that the Risperdal was more effective at controlling both my residual psychotic symptoms and my weight. At the end of the study, I was given the opportunity to receive Risperdal for some six months at no cost, an offer I gratefully accepted.

Since that time, though I have indeed gained more weight while on Risperdal (in fact more in total than I ever did on Clozaril), I have never found a better medication for keeping my mood and psychotic symptoms at bay. Risperdal, in combination with Depakote, Anafranil, and Cogentin as a "side effect med"/mild antidepressant (I also take fish oil capsules for their mood-leveling Omega-3 ingredients, and thyroid medications to compensate for my hypothyroidism, which perhaps developed secondary to lithium treatment), makes it possible for me to feel like a whole, well person—more often than not. As does my therapeutic relationship with my new psychotherapist, a sensitive and wise soul whom I never doubt is on my side, and with my new psychiatrist, a world-renowned mood disorders expert highly (and rightfully) recommended to me after the doctor I started working with during my hospitalization in 1991 (which I hope was my last one ever) moved out of the Washington, DC, area.

MEDS I HAVE KNOWN

As I've described my two hospitalizations in depth, it must be clear that I have a love-hate relationship with medications, or "meds" as my fellow consumers and I call them. Tofranil, known generically as imipramine, was the first psychotropic medication I ever took, for my emerging depression in 1984. A tricyclic, or old-style antidepressant, it served to catapult me out of stuporous depression in a matter of weeks. It continued to work quite well for a while, but later switched me into my first hypomania and probably started my rapid-cycling merry-go-round. Several years after I started taking tricyclics, a theory was advanced that such medications could cause or accelerate mood cycling, and many psychiatrists continue to hold this view today.

Mellaril, a typical (or older) antipsychotic and one of the only class of neuroleptics available at the time, was added to my regimen while I was in the hospital in 1984 to control my delusions, and was fairly effective at a low dose but made me extremely sleepy. My system couldn't handle more than 25 mg per day, and as my psychosis soon stabilized, I was then tapered off the med.

A few months later, I was tried on lithium. Four words—hand tremor, scarring acne. But as the first mood stabilizer I ever took, it was reasonably efficacious. Tegretol was the next mood stabilizer I tried after my lithium tremor hindered my ability to work with my hands aliquoting blood at the NIMH lab; it stopped the mania but left me depressed.

Then I began rapid-cycling and ended up responding much better to Depakote, which is now the front-line choice rather than lithium for us rapid-cyclers. Depakote has exacerbated the packing on of pounds over the years, but has been my saving grace as a mood stabilizer. It isn't perfect for staving off the ultra-rapid mood cycles, but it helps me feel like my real self, and I take it to this day. Depakote and I are comfortable together, I guess you'd say.

A few years into college, when it became apparent that my depressive episodes had taken a complicated course, I started taking Nardil. This med, an MAOI (monoamine oxidase inhibitor, an older and less-prescribed class of antidepressants) took off the pounds but overshot me into brain-buzz hypomania. If there had been any doubt that my illness was a form of bipolar disorder, treatment with Nardil sealed the deal. My family members commented that "Shannon, you don't seem like yourself." "Yeah, you're so irritable." "Why'd you snap at me? You never do that!"

The offending Nardil was soon removed from my personal formulary in favor of more tricyclics; the one I stuck with and still take today, in a very small dose, is Anafranil (clomipramine is the generic name). Before trying Anafranil, while I was in college, an extremely high dose of desipramine (as prescribed for me) precipitated a toxic whole-body tremor that led to me falling in the middle of the street and getting a mouth infection that almost spread up to my brain. I was treated at Georgetown University Hospital for the infection with surgery. (For some reason, the administration of anesthesia terrified me so that I kept crying out in agitation, "No! Please don't put that mask over me!" This caused the attending surgeon to remark to his eager interns as I cowered under the anesthesia mask, "Remember, this patient has bipolar disorder—this is a good example of how this illness can present.")

Trimipramine, another one of several tricyclic antidepressants I took when first diagnosed, caused an itchy rash on my hands and arms. Later, Prozac, one of the newer class of antidepressants, the SSRIs (selective serotonin reuptake inhibitors), was prescribed briefly for me during my junior year of college (1988-1989). This drug didn't agree with me, though—it left me unable to sleep or cry, and may have exacerbated my cutting behavior, as will be discussed later.

Xanax and Ativan, anxiolytic meds prescribed at various times during my college years to alleviate my anxiety on a PRN or "as needed" basis, unfortunately always made me feel spaced out to an unpleasant degree—so far out of cognitive control that I avoid benzodiazepines like the plague now. Intolerable as panic episodes may seem, I prefer enduring them to the greater fear that results from taking Ativan and suddenly finding myself in black oblivion.

As my paranoia over people talking about me or reading my mind developed after college, my psychiatrist prescribed the typical antipsychotic, Stelazine, which gave me severe parkinsonian side effects. In short, taking it caused me to be so stiff that I "looked like a robot," according to my family. I also remember time passing painfully slowly (paradoxically taking forever to tick by) because of what in retrospect was probably internal akithesia (inner restlessness or disquiet). When it became clear that I simply could not tolerate the Stelazine, I was prescribed Loxitane, which seemed to mellow out some of the paranoia, though I only took this med for a few weeks. Remember that this was occurring in 1990, right before the advent of second-generation antipsychotics, so other alternatives didn't really exist at the time.

Once I was in the hospital, the best stopgap measure my new psychiatrist devised for me, as I've mentioned, was to start me on Clozaril, the first of the atypical antipsychotics. This "miracle drug" started working almost as soon as I took it, dramatically improving my suicidal agitation, continual self-injurious behavior, mood swings, and paranoia. Though I quickly recovered from my affective psychosis and returned to work, at times I stumbled through the hours in a drowsy fog. Clozaril, despite its vital benefits, had several aforementioned drawbacks. It caused me to gain 50 pounds, drool, and sleep through the work day—if I could get up on time in the first place.

Risperdal, on the other hand, has been my saving grace for alleviating paranoid ideation and anxiety and, to a lesser extent, my mood cycles for the past 16 or so years. I switched from Clozaril to Risperdal during a double-blind coded protocol in 1994, having finally given up on overcoming the extreme sedation, drooling, and weight gain precipitated by Clozaril. At first I found myself mildly depressed, but once the Clozaril was totally depleted from my system and the Risperdal accumulated to a therapeutic level, I felt I had finally gotten myself back again. While on Risperdal, as I've written, I have gained more than 100 pounds, but whenever I've tried to replace it with another antipsychotic, the results have without exception been discouraging.

I've experienced a great deal of frustration and even a sense of hopelessness about managing my excess weight; at several points I have turned to medications to control this. Geodon and Abilify, the two "weight-neutral" antipsychotics I've tried in place of Risperdal, both catapulted me into a frightening mixed mania. On both of these antipsychotics, I thankfully lost weight but paid for it with an agitated brain buzz that left me unable to sleep more than four hours a night and knotted me up with anxiety. Abilify in particular caused me to become so paranoid at work that I became convinced my Asian friend in the next cubicle was talking about me in Chinese when she called her family, and I felt so afraid of everyone else's supposed malevolent intentions toward me that I rarely dared to walk down the hall past colleagues' doors.

The next remedy we tried was Topamax, a weight-loss inducing anticonvulsant otherwise known (by consumers at any rate) as "Dopamax," because it addled my hitherto-taken-for-granted intellect to the point that I couldn't find simple words like "umbrella" or "doorknob." On the up side, it did help me start losing weight for the first time in years. Still, since I've always identified myself so much with my cognitive abilities, I felt less like a person than like an aphasic moron on Topamax and chose to be fat and smart rather than thin and stupid.

Still, as much as I dislike my weight gain, I would never become noncompliant with my medications, because I know what could happen if I stopped taking them. The consequences of not being medicated—such as death!—are far more dire than those of taking the meds.

Although I don't see noncompliance as the answer to medication woes, I do view trials of new medications as a possible solution for myself. Because of my continual determination to better myself and my control over my illness, I am quite proactive in asking my psychiatrist to supervise my trials of new medications that may alleviate weight gain, or sedation, or may help remediate the troubling aphasia that persists despite my not having taken Topamax for several years.

My doctor, who thankfully works with me as a partner in recovery instead of as a helpless patient to be dictated to, has always encouraged me to try out new medications as they become available. He assured me during my last appointment that, as pharmaceutical science advances, the likelihood of smarter drugs being developed, with more targeted receptor binding to maximize psychotropic effects while minimizing side effects, is quite high. As long as I have that hope, I will never give up on finding the best medications possible for me. I know that, for all their limitations, psychotropic medicines are crucial for maintaining recovery—at least for me.

As of this writing I'm on four psychotropic meds: Depakote and Risperdal, my good old mainstays for so many years; Cogentin, which has been my "side effect med" for quite some time, and which has the strange effect of causing mild depression if I run out and am unable to get to the pharmacy; and a very low dose of Anafranil, a tricyclic that helps at least somewhat with my obsessive thoughts about all the things I've done wrong, but that can trigger psychosis if I take more than 50 mg per day. I also take Omega-3 fish oil, which helps level out my moods, and vitamin B6 helps contain my premenstrual dysphoria. I take Synthroid and Cytomel for my hypothyroidism; I don't physically feel any good effects, but my TSH and

T4 levels are back to normal when I take them. In short—meds: can't live with 'em, can't live without 'em.

Reading my account of the meds I've taken, you might suppose that I despise psychotropic medications. While I do despise their side effects, I probably owe my life to the health-restoring properties of modern psychiatric drugs—to them along with the encouragement and support of my loved ones, psychotherapy, creative outlets like art and writing, and my relationship with God. It is possible that without my mood stabilizers and antipsychotic, I would be dead now instead of writing this book. Suicide would surely have claimed me had not the judicious and prompt administration of psychotropics rapidly rescued me from danger in times of acute crises.

I'm certain that sometime in the hopefully not too distant future, scientists and psychiatrists, not to mention we patients, will look back on our present era of medication as barbaric, the way we now view lobotomies and the administration of ECT (electroconvulsive therapy) as it was practiced in its earliest days. Maybe mental illnesses will be cured in the future—and note that I write "cured," not "treated"—by a more natural means or process that involves acknowledging the oneness of mind and body, that avoids blaming the victim, and that doesn't bring with it the inevitable $@#% side effects that cause too many of us to abandon our medications now. Of course, the means of addressing mental illness in future times may actually involve gene therapy or "smart drugs" or some other purely biological treatment. But my wish is that holistic healing will be used in some way for us as well.

A WEIGHTY PROBLEM

I've often wondered whether holistic methods can help with weight loss, and have vowed to research this avenue to better health. Current theory about mind-body unity might help me regain my self-respect—and even might have helped me before my identity as a psychiatric consumer began!

Something strange: I now realize that back then, as a 110-pound young woman with long, golden-blonde hair and sad blue eyes, I was actually—dare I say it—pretty. I just didn't believe it and in fact thought myself hideously ugly and fat. Now that my short hair has darkened to a mousy, dark dirty blonde and my round face is cushioned in the same fat that pillows over my 200+ pound body, I would give anything to have back that attractive young form.

Well, I guess I wouldn't give *anything* after all. It all boils down to a most vexing choice: would I rather be well, or would I rather be thin? In this era of atypical antipsychotics, various ones of which I've been taking for the past 20 years, people like me have few options other than to beef up on meds to the degree that our health is seriously compromised, not to mention our self-esteem. I don't think that many psychiatrists, not to mention families, friends, and bystanders, understand quite how difficult it is to lose med-induced weight (Depakote and Anafranil have contributed their fair share of my weight gain, along with the Clozaril and Risperdal). For the past 20 years, I've lost and regained the same 20 or 40 pounds—and that isn't nearly all of the excess weight I need to shed to look the way I did at 17. While Weight Watchers is a very effective program if followed religiously, I must have joined and rejoined the program seven times or so over the past 10-15 years.

"People with schizophrenia [and other psychotic disorders] tend not to be motivated to address the problems brought on by their obesity," I read in some psychiatric journal or other. Actually, I've read words to that effect several times, and each time I have, I've felt guilty because I know it's true. I think I know the reason, at least my reason, though: when I'm slogged down with multiple sedating meds in my system and my symptoms include lack of energy and lack of self-esteem, it's awfully hard to "just do it" and go to a gym on a weekend when I'd rather sleep in, or eat carrots while craving doughnuts for their carbohydrates and serotonin. Not to mention that the odds are stacked against my losing weight because my meds slow my metabolism and sometimes increase my appetite.

And yet, time and again, I've heeded the wake-up call that looking with disgust in the mirror sounds, and I've tried to lose weight and exercise. My dilemma is that, at least so far, I've never kept my good efforts and intentions going. I recently started Weight Watchers again and feel committed to eating better and starting to exercise again (although I know I'll always crave chocolate at a certain time of the month, and I'll probably never love exercising). As of today, I've had several good days and feel positive about my new lifestyle. Let's just hope I really will make it a *lifestyle* and not just a temporary diet that I later abandon (only to gain all the weight back and then some).

I know I'm at risk for diabetes and heart disease with my obesity; I know that people look at me now (some are outspoken enough to wound me with their jeers as I walk down the street) with a much different attitude than in my thin days—and sometimes this makes me furious enough that I almost stop taking the meds to reclaim myself as I once was. But only almost.

I found out the hard way—over the span of three days during college—that stopping my meds abruptly turns my life into a waking nightmare. When I stopped my cocktail of antipsychotics, mood stabilizers, and antidepressants, I was gripped almost immediately by paranoia, painful agitation, and finally a depression whose stupor approached that of my first episode. I can remember glancing in the mirror during that short but agonizing period and suddenly dissolving into tears at my utter rottenness. I can remember holing up in our dorm's student lounge in the middle of the night, covering myself with blankets, and cutting into my wrists and arms with shards of glass I had found in the parking lot. (Of course I didn't clean the dirt off the glass first.) I remember convincing myself that I didn't deserve to eat, similar to my behavior during my first (and worst) depression. So my noncompliance stint ended, and I resignedly resumed taking the meds again. I have ever since.

It still arouses rage in me from time to time, though, knowing that millions of other people with psychotic disorders across the country (and probably around the world) like me have no choice other than to get fat if they want to stay well. In fact, as I understand it, significant weight gain on atypical antipsychotics actually predicts robust response to the drugs. And suffice it to say that I've responded extremely successfully to the Clozaril and Risperdal that I've taken and continue to take. Well, so have lots of other people I know—and this just isn't fair. Bipolar disorder or schizophrenia is hard enough without the added difficulty of being unhealthy, looking unattractive, and feeling inferior. After all, it's still apparently OK to make fun of fat people.

And before I lumped all this weight on, I was just as guilty as any bystander on the street who has mumbled hurtful comments about my "fat sticky-out ass." I never made or would ever dream of making catcalls to overweight people, but I carried the same prejudices and malicious judgments about those I figured were too "lazy" or "sloppy" to take care of themselves and lose the weight. I mean, how hard could it be?

This was my reasoning when I inhabited a relatively thin, healthy body as a teenager, since it was effortless then for me to maintain a healthy weight. Well, now I know better. As I've watched my stomach pouch out to the point where a passerby once asked if I were pregnant; as I've prodded the gruesome cellulite that's accumulated at an alarming rate on my jiggly arms and thighs; as my breasts have expanded from well-proportioned to uncomfortably ample and become fodder for suggestive taunts from men on the street—I've learned what it feels like to be an object instead of a person. An object for ridicule, not desire. Is it any wonder that it's hard for those of us burdened with this little "side effect" to drag ourselves out from under it and become thin and healthy again?

Being a med-made fat person is frightening, too. In the past 18 or 19 years, I haven't merely gained a ton of weight; also my health has begun to suffer seriously. Thank God, my glucose has always been fine—usually between 80 and 90—but I've developed worrisome shortness of breath, heart palpitations, and prominent edema in my ankles, along with arthritis of several years' duration. Because of all these problems, I am no longer able to walk any distance longer than a few city blocks without wrenching back pain and gasps for breath. I feel very remorseful when I remember the relative ease with which my husband and I walked for hours in an international garden in Montreal seven years ago on our honeymoon.

And don't even mention running! That's been a joke for years as far as I'm concerned. I live in fear of the day when I gasp and keel over in a heart attack—I've had three scares during which I had trouble breathing, mild chest pain, and palpitations. In all three cases, my EKG and chest X-rays turned out fine, and it was determined that I'd experienced only a panic attack, but I am now beginning to panic about the state of my ticker!

So, you say, *Dumbass, why aren't you doing anything about this problem?!* And there's no easy answer for that question. It seems that the more doctors and nosy laypeople tell me to get off my duff, start exercising, eat this, don't eat that, the more I unconsciously resist. And I am normally a very compliant, eager-to-please person; I can't figure out why I would knowingly endanger my health.

I suppose one reason is that I *have* tried, unsuccessfully, over and over again, to lose weight and exercise, but I've never been able to sustain the practice for more than a few weeks at a time. Perhaps another reason is that on some hidden level I want to sabotage my well-being because of a wish to passively damage myself. I truly hope I am not doing the latter, because I like to tell myself I've successfully pushed aside my self-destructive urges. Resisting urges to hurt myself in any way is an endeavor at which I thought I had succeeded.

Whatever the reasons, I now feel a kinship to other heavy people out there, whether psychiatric clients or not. All of us undergo continual harassment for our excess weight, scorn that is *almost* as noxious as the untreated symptoms of my bipolar disorder. As I said, I've chosen mental health at the price of physical health. I know peers who've made the opposite choice, surrendering their sanity to maintain a healthy physique, and I can't blame them. Maybe I and others like me are not trying to hurt ourselves so much as trying *not* to harm ourselves, in "weighing" our options to make these excruciatingly difficult decisions.

SELF-INJURIOUS BEHAVIORS

My last statement does not mean that I haven't carried out other self-destructive activities, unfortunately. Moving on to another type of medication-related self-harming behavior, one which I engaged in for 15 or 16 years altogether, I should add that my aforementioned wrist-cutting could possibly have been triggered by my use of Prozac during my junior year in college—although I had laid the foundation for self-harm long before. As I've discussed, though I'd been banging my head and occasionally striking myself with belts since childhood, I had never really cut my skin with blades even during my worst, initial depression in 1984—even then, I'd felt so listless I'd mostly just stuck myself with pins to draw blood.

My vulnerable nervous system extends to my emotional hypersensitivity to perceived rejection from important people in my life. Here my overactive imagination, along with my tendency toward paranoia, comes into play as well. Until quite recently, I've been too quick to interpret an offhand remark from a friend who's had a bad day as a personal affront. After this misperception, I would proceed to (a) cry; (b) wonder what I did to make her or him hate me so much; and (c) analyze every word of the conversation to death to ferret out exactly what I'd done wrong. Back in my early 20s, before I stopped the self-mutilation, I also would usually proceed to cut myself as well in response to the imagined rejection.

Once I was prescribed Prozac, when the antidepressant first came on the market in the late 1980s, I soon felt uncomfortable psychic effects. I was unable to sleep, when previously my meds had sedated me; disturbingly, I also found myself unable to cry, even when I was upset and knew that I needed to release pent-up emotion.

One night during that Prozac era, alone in my dorm room, feeling distraught over some trivial interpersonal crisis but unable to release any tears, I suddenly grabbed for my razor and made a half-hearted slash across my arm to see whether I could relieve my mental angst that way. Lo and behold, this method worked, at least providing a temporary fix, and I proceeded to cut myself, often at the slightest provocation, for the next four or five years.

Many theories exist as to why people like me engage, or have engaged, in the practice of deliberately hurting themselves, particularly through self-cutting. I can only speak for myself, and I've pondered this behavior thoroughly to untangle its gnarled roots. The truest answer I can give is that most of the time, when I cut, I did so to punish myself for having made someone stop loving me (as I believed, however erroneously). Another piece of my particular puzzle falls into place with my realization that although I was punishing myself, I also was angry at the other person, who I thought had rejected me; and it was my pattern at the time to turn all negative emotions toward others (like anger) against myself in retroflection.

I also might explain that I was substituting physical pain for emotional pain I didn't want to feel. Except that's not exactly right, because most of the time when I cut, I felt nothing physically and even seemed to dissociate, feeling somehow outside myself. On the other hand, I did achieve a calming sense of numbness, both emotional and physical, and perhaps that soothing emptiness, carried on the flowing tide of endorphins, is what I ultimately craved. Nothing existed in that moment except the sleepy wooziness of a knife and my wrist (or occasionally my arm or leg) starting to drip with blood. In fact, I often went to sleep after cutting and cleaning myself up.

It has often been assumed that the reason people cut themselves is to be histrionic and announce to their world their suffering. That was never true for me. I always used to cut in secret, hide my scars, and not tell anyone that I had done so—until the summer of 1991, when I became so sick that I asked for help and admitted my behavior. Otherwise, I was not looking for attention, just a way to release the turbulent feelings that so overwhelmed me after any hint of interpersonal conflict.

Another misconception is that people who cut themselves are never suicidal, but only wish to hurt themselves superficially. In my mind that boundary was sometimes hazy. Often when I cut my wrists, I began with the intention of making a little cut to feel better, lulled by the hypnotic motion of the blade in my hand. If, however, I was unable to completely suppress my emotional anguish, I might impulsively try to escape the global pain of existence by cutting a little deeper . . . Who is to say what was "delicate self-cutting" and what was the beginning of a suicide attempt? I know I was never lucid enough at such a point to figure it out. Luckily I never did make a serious attempt, because at a critical point I would get scared of the mess I was making, which would abruptly "sober" me up. I would then clean my cut and seek escape through sleep instead.

During that interval of my life, I actually may have been physically addicted to the cutting, a theory that makes sense; some psychiatrists believe cutting the skin ritualistically and repetitively leads to endorphin release. I do know that at the time self-injury was my first and most-depended-on choice of coping "skills," and it took years to grow beyond hurting myself as a paradoxical means of protecting myself from harm. How sad that I—or any young person, for our ranks are swelling—would have to resort to self-inflicted violence just to fill the human need for comfort and contact that I was unable to find in bonds with other people. Self-harm is fundamentally intertwined with lonely self-hatred.

And yet, slowly, with therapy and time, the healthy part within me was able to assert itself all the while the toxic part led me to ritualistically hurt myself. By that time in college, I had just begun to focus on psychology and on ultimately becoming what psychiatrist E. Fuller Torrey calls "not a mental health professional, but a mental *illness* professional." That path has at times been daunting, but the healing I've experienced as I've (mostly) stopped my self-harming behaviors has prepared me for helping other people who struggle with similar issues.

Still, in my first session with my current psychotherapist, I found myself telling her with angry tears in my eyes, "I know I have to deal with this bipolar disorder, but that's just no excuse for not having achieved everything I should have in life. I always think of Dr. Kay Redfield Jamison [she's my role model, the thin and brilliant bipolar 'mental illness professional'] and I have to tell myself, like it or not, *'You're no Kay Jamison!'* So maybe I should just give up."

And she replied, "But you don't have to be Kay Jamison. You just have to be the best Shannon you can be. And no one else but you can do that." Well, I'm beginning to believe she may be right, but I've taken quite a circuitous route to make this realization.

Again I crash into the brick wall of my fear of not being perfect, but in this case, of not being the best consumer-provider possible. Why can't I just accept that other bipolar people—other *people*—may be more energetic and effective, smarter and more creative, more generous and giving, than I—*and that's OK?*

*   *   *   *

Since I wrote the previous paragraph, I've taken a hiatus for several days from working on this manuscript. During that time I attended a family celebration that left me feeling considerable tension over what a "dysfunctional" family I thought I belonged to (although in reality I know we're not dysfunctional, just larger than most other families, making us seem more chaotic).

The next day I looked in the mirror while dressing and became disgusted with what I saw. "F___ the whole world!" I yelled in frustration—and beat my two fists against either side of my head five or six times. Immediately afterward I calmed down, but started crying because I had broken my record (since 1991) of not hurting myself. At least I hadn't cut. But I realized that family gatherings, coupled with the inescapable fact of my massive weight gain, as well as the emotions stirred up despite my best intentions by writing about my past, are powerful forces that can lead me to the edge. I have taken extra care since then not to step over that edge. I never again want to regress to where I've been while at my sickest.

My husband Tom, my psychiatrist, and my psychotherapist have been supportive without making an overly big fuss about my impulsive hurtful acts. While I might wail over the fear that I'm returning to my self-destructive ways of 15 years ago, they have all sensibly urged me to be watchful, but at the same time to find ways to express anger against my family instead of against myself—and to lose the weight so I'll no longer feel repulsed by myself. I know they're right.

At a recent Weight Watchers meeting, the leader made an extraordinarily wise, apt analogy that applies to me on several levels. She said that when a baby starts walking, she progresses slowly from crawling to toddling along, often falling down and beginning over again. But no one says to the baby, "You're falling a lot. I don't think this walking stuff is for you—you'd better go back to crawling." No, because the parents want their baby to walk, and the baby wants to walk too. Crashing and getting back up again is just the natural order of life—kind of like mood cycles, the ebb and flow of highs and lows. So too with me and my tumbles.

THE STING OF STIGMA

However, no matter how determined those of us who live with psychiatric conditions are to stay mentally healthy and avoid self-harm, society and the public at large often perpetrate just as much harm against us. Stigma—discrimination—condescension—injustice. I've found that everyone I've talked to who lives with one of these illnesses has a story about having been stigmatized or discriminated against. I'm lucky—I've been ridiculed and misunderstood a couple of times by ignorant people, but that's all that has happened to me. Other people I know have lost jobs; been denied housing, insurance, or health care; or become estranged from family members and others they cared about. Fortunately for me, most of my colleagues have been supportive or at least tolerant if I disclosed my illness—which for the most part I have.

However, when I was in college, disclosing my disability to a roommate one year turned out to be a mistake. I remember my earnest explanation to her of my symptoms and need to take medication—as I saw it, I was helpfully forewarning her in case I should take a tumble later in the school year. Of course, that winter I did decompensate into a dozy, apathetic depression that I tried to sleep through. Her comment to a friend, heard dimly through a fog of sleep, penetrated my apathy: "Oh, that Shannon—she's such a psycho! She told me all about her psychiatric problems at the beginning of the year and I was like, 'I don't want to hear it.'" And all along I'd thought she'd accepted, if not exactly liked, me. But that no longer has the power to hurt me; I think she was just a bit ignorant and perhaps scared.

My more recent experience with stigma has left a more lasting scar, though. Some years ago, while I was working at NIMH (National Institute of Mental Health) before the regulation was enacted that members of a particular institute may not participate in a study done by their own institute, I took part in a study on schizophrenia, having recently been diagnosed by my psychiatrist as schizoaffective disorder, bipolar type. I ended up being categorized by the study psychiatrist as bipolar (and have been so diagnosed ever since), and so my data were not included in the final analysis for the study. Nevertheless, a research chart, complete with documentation covering my past psychiatric hospitalization and outpatient records, was generated and stored.

Several years later, after my NIMH branch dissolved, I ended up coming to work for the particular branch that conducted that study, becoming first a research assistant, later a recruiter and "consumer outreach coordinator." My new branch, like most others throughout the entire National Institutes of Health (NIH), employs fresh college graduates who stay for one to two years to do post-baccalaureate research and then go on to graduate or medical school. One year, we hired a young person with a sharp wit and a predilection for playing practical jokes on colleagues, someone with whom I thought I got along rather well.

Until the afternoon when, while I entered data at my computer, I suddenly heard this employee laughing with two other post-bac hires in the adjoining office—over my chart! "Oh my God—she used to bang her head on the wall." "So she's *bipolar*"—spoken in the same tone as though I were leprous. "She doesn't seem like it . . ." "Yeah, but she sure seems like *something's* wrong with her!" "I showed her a list of antipsychotic medications and she told me she used to be on half of them!" (It was true; I had naively made that comment, believing that my colleague was sympathetic to my condition.)

Hearing this, I was frozen to my desk in hurt and outrage. How I wanted to march over to the other office and demand, "Give me my chart back right now. How dare you make fun of me for having an illness that any one of you could develop at any time?" But my cowardice and humiliation paralyzed me. Why should I have been so humiliated, I now wonder. Bipolar disorder is still part of the human condition, an illness like cancer or heart disease or epilepsy. I'm still a person just as they are, just as is everyone. My problem simply happens to affect my mind and my emotions instead of only my body, that's all.

Luckily, since the episode at work, my experiences of discrimination have been few. However, recently my husband Tom and I investigated the purchase of life insurance so that either of us can provide for ourself in the case of the other's death. I spent time calling the major life insurance companies: Nationwide, TIAA-CREF, Northwestern, and MetLife, and divulging medical information that should be none of the phone representatives' business, but is because it would factor into the quotes they gave me.

I quickly discovered that insurance companies are very interested in my height and weight, no matter how embarrassed I may be to reveal them. And the simple statement that, "Both my husband and I have bipolar disorder" tends to stop them in their tracks. "Oh, well, that's going to make your premiums higher, if we can insure you at all" is the invariable response. In fact, I waited several weeks for a quote after revealing our bipolar disorder to one of the agents at Northwestern. I would have thought they'd be happy to get our money, but such was not the case.

Right after agents would tell me Tom's and my premiums would be higher, they put us in "risk categories." Tom got put in Category B because he had just quit smoking in addition to his mood disorder. But I wound up in Category F even though I've never smoked—I can only assume it's because of my morbid obesity ("morbid" is probably the operative word).

The agents all wanted to know what medications we're on as well. Come to think of it, probably divulging that I'm taking an atypical antipsychotic, Risperdal (in addition to a mood stabilizer, antidepressant, antiparkinsonian agent, and thyroid replacement), gave them pause. It wasn't a good sign of my insurability that I'm on a bona fide "crazy" med, in contrast to Tom's more benign mood stabilizer and antidepressant. The fact that I've been hospitalized twice also seemed to be more significant than the fact that the last hospitalization was nearly 20 years ago, let alone that I'm successfully holding down a full-time job and have a master's degree and post-master's certificate.

I would guess that going through the process of obtaining life insurance is one of the least enjoyable events for anyone. It felt doubly unpleasant for Tom and me, though, in light of the demeaning way some of the insurance company representatives interacted with us.

I will say that of all the people we spoke with, I was actually impressed with the matter-of-fact, non-condescending phone manner of the TIAA-CREF agent. Yes, he did ask all the inevitable questions, but he received the answers with equanimity and spent at least half an hour on the phone with me running quotes for all different sorts of level term insurance, for both Tom and me. At no time did his voice take on that all-too-familiar superior tone; he was completely polite and very helpful. We at one point assumed we'd buy our policies from him.

But isn't it ironic—despite the friendly phone manner of the TIAA-CREF insurance agent, the company as a whole proved to be considerably less consumer-friendly. Both Tom and I received thin white envelopes (just like college rejection letters) from the insurance company, separately informing us that "due to the information provided us by Dr. ___ [our respective psychiatrists], we are unable to offer you a policy at this time."

Reading between those lines wasn't very hard—the fine folks at TIAA-CREF felt that our pre-existing conditions, shall we say, sharply curtailed our insurability.

Luckily, a few days later, we received quite generous (meaning low-premium) offers of term life insurance from another company, MetLife. As it happened, the representative from this company developed more than a phone relationship with us as time passed. He came out to our house from his office 30 miles away, discussed our health risks frankly but compassionately, and continued to stay in contact with Tom and me as the underwriting proceeded. Several weeks later, he personally returned to our house to deliver our insurance policies. MetLife: we're satisfied customers.

Another form of stigma and its effects also happen to people like me with psychiatric conditions, at times, when being treated by mental health professionals of every type. It seems to me that's the dirty secret of being in the mental health field: you're allegedly working in this profession to help empower mental health consumers, while in fact you are robbing us of our power. Too often the initial fierce desire to free us from the chains of our illnesses burns out to embers of the former enthusiasm, and "How can I help you help yourself today?" becomes, "Have you taken your meds yet? Don't think you can get away with cheeking them today."

While studying for my M.A. in art therapy at George Washington University and participating in an internship at an acclaimed military hospital with several psychiatric wards, I regularly attended clinical consult liaison meetings. I felt out of place often, not only as the lone civilian, but mainly because I was keeper of the secret that I was a consumer in disguise, one of "them."

How can I forget the day an officer and psychiatrist-in-training, upon hearing another clinician describe getting hugged by a client, saying, "A hug from a patient—uggghhh" with an accompanying disgusted shiver? Or forget the way the other would-be doctors of the psyche laughed in camaraderie and shared revulsion? Making me feel revolted toward myself, all hideous heft and tremoring hands.

Much more recently (in 2009), I underwent a counseling internship with the National Institute on Alcohol Abuse and Alcoholism (NIAAA), learning how to run cognitive behavioral therapy groups and conduct behavioral assessments for people in recovery from addictions. My supervisor, a psychiatric nurse and licensed counselor with many years of experience under her belt, proved to be immensely instrumental and encouraging in helping me learn the skills needed to help the people we counsel.

However, in what became a typical reaction for me, I found myself tearing up slightly from time to time when listening to people's stories of their dark days, perhaps because they reminded me of my own depressions (though I have never had a substance abuse problem), and perhaps because of my own easily aroused sensitivity. I have always been preternaturally attuned to my own and others' feelings, even if my knowledge of social conventions—in other words, how to respond appropriately to those feelings—has not always been up to par. This oversensitivity probably explains in part why I shrivel in the face of someone's anger or even mild disapproval. It also—along with my general people-pleasing tendencies—accounts for my desire to listen to and minister to people in mental pain. Too, my ever-ready empathy explains my wish to magically "fix" the personal problems of my friends, family—and clients.

Even today, in my relatively stable state of mind, I frequently tear up when a friend confiding in me starts crying herself, because empathically I am feeling her emotions through her. This eye-watering occasionally became something of a hindrance the first time I worked at a hospital conducting psychiatric art therapy groups in 1999. Every now and then, a client would describe her or his artwork, or talk about a problem with anguish in her or his voice, and I would suddenly have to explain that my eyes were watering "because my allergies are acting up." (Rare among Washingtonians, I do not have allergies.)

How I wish I had been courageous enough to admit that I was tearing up because the client's story touched my heart. I could have explained this with no need to further reveal any shared identity as a mental health consumer (although at times I've wished that were permitted as well—it might engender better "accurate empathy"). This hair-trigger emotionality, along with my fear of telling my coworkers that I was a psychiatric consumer, contributed to my leaving an art therapy job when I received a promotion at NIMH.

In the case of my more recent internship, I did disclose my emotionality and its likely reasons to my supervisor, and then arrived the next day at the clinic to overhear—at least I thought I did; I know I have a tendency to misperceive and misinterpret people's remarks—a conversation among several of the staff about my flaws as a potential counselor. I was "too sensitive" and had "no boundaries" and "got upset too easily," and they doubted I would make it as a counselor.

Immediately, I felt humiliated and furious at myself, as well as deeply concerned that in fact I never would be able to be a counselor and fulfill my life's calling, despite my ardent wishes to do just that. In the intervening days I've analyzed and overanalyzed the conversation and plumbed the depths of my heart, trying to determine whether I can become a therapist as I feel called to do. I've determined that I want to show them that I can do exactly that, and that I will try my hardest to lay aside my feelings and concentrate on serving my clients instead.

From time to time I have struggled with the fear that I will never be able to become a "regular" or mainstream mental health professional because of the way I wear my heart on my sleeve, that I'll have to work only among the peer-run mental health network. Nothing is wrong with this type of endeavor—far from it, as I can see strong evidence that the consumer-run mental health movement is rapidly growing in credibility and power. In the peer-run arena, my identity as a psychiatric consumer would abet rather than limit my ability to act as an empathic counselor.

Still, perhaps for the wrong reasons (though I haven't been able to tease these out yet), I feel a drive to establish myself in the mainstream mental health network and to prove that I can practice counseling and art therapy just as well as the "normals." I do see one potentially positive aspect to this aspiration: I could thereby give hope to other consumers striving to be providers, or "prosumers," because I believe (as do many other peers) that a viable mental health system must include all of us on an equal basis.

It's no surprise that we've all internalized the prejudice we've faced as people treated for mental illnesses. And I think that this self-stigma is the most insidious and perhaps the worst kind of all. Our own judgments against ourselves wound us even more deeply than others' judgments, because they keep us from pursuing full lives. How many times have I told myself that I didn't deserve to date; and later, to marry; have a rewarding job; have my own home; in general, be happy—because I was a lower life form than other, *normal* people? Yes, my reaction to treatment professionals' discrimination has been anger, but my reaction to my own stigma has more often than not been shame.

I've experienced both sides of the therapeutic couch, becoming in turn both consumer and provider. With my dual expertise, I'd like to educate other professionals about the dignity that we have, those of us with depression or bipolar disorder or borderline personality disorder or schizophrenia or . . . We're not as different from you providers as you might imagine: I'm living proof of that. This passionate belief fuels my need to be an advocate for everyone like me.

MY EVOLUTION OF GOD

I know I could not have arrived at my powerful drive for consumer advocacy without the comforting belief in a universal moral force supporting my efforts. All the same, I'm sure it's equally clear that I grew up deathly afraid of a different deity: God the Almighty Father. The terror-inducing ideas I held about Him were molded in part from the clay of my Roman Catholic upbringing. Much more influential, though, were the dark machinations of my own disturbed mind. Faulty wiring caused me to interpret episodes (such as the religion class about Abraham and Isaac) as direct salvos from a furious God bent on harming if not killing me when I might least expect it.

Nevertheless, I shouldn't make it sound as though I was in constant fear for my life as I grew from a child to a young woman. My reality testing mechanism did work to some degree, and my dark and bright moods cycled so that I experienced considerable periods of relief from my fear of God. Still, in those days I always found it much easier to tremble before Him than to love Him.

As I began to recover from my first episode of depression, however, I found my relationship with God transforming. For the first time in my life, I was able to conceive of a Higher Power who held me in the palm of His (or Her!) hand instead of wanting to destroy me, who offered joyful peace if only I would reach out for it. Maybe my depression, agitation, and psychosis had been sent to me not as a curse but as a blessing, as an opportunity for growth and renewal. As I moved from plotting for death to yearning for life, I found that this emergence from my spiritual chrysalis fueled my ardor to improve the well-being of those who live with similar illnesses.

The ritual form my religious or spiritual practice has taken has evolved as I've traveled from the territory of sick to well. As I've mentioned, I was raised Roman Catholic, with all the attendant trappings such as solemn nuns and priests, ornate churches suffused with clove incense, rosaries, warnings about adhering to the One True Religion and abstaining from premarital hand-holding (OK, that's a slight exaggeration!), and plaid school uniforms. I traversed this world with head bowed in unquestioning, childlike faith, all the way through college.

Then, in my late 20s I gravitated toward a wider religious exploration, which led me to Unitarian Universalism (UU), a type of spirituality I feel more comfortable with today, though I must admit I am a Unitarian in name rather than in regular practice. Although I've heard some people dismiss Unitarianism as coldly intellectual, for me it has always been emotionally comforting in a way Catholicism had not been. Unitarians not only don't believe in hell, they believe that God would never damn anyone to hell because of her (or his, or its) great love. (Actually, a Unitarian doesn't even have to believe in God, though all the ones I've met believe in good.)

What many Unitarians—and I, usually—do hold as a creed is, basically, whatever helps us the most on a personal spiritual level. But all Unitarians are committed to social justice, which is one of the most valuable tenets of the faith for me and the principle that first attracted me to the tradition. Respect for all individuals and respect for the earth and all its living beings are paramount. Any Unitarian congregation welcomes people who are poor; who are marginalized; who are gay or lesbian; who are of any ethnic background; who are mentally ill; who are in any kind of need—in short, anyone.

I've attended several UU churches in the Washington, DC, area, and what they all seem to have in common is a joyous outlook on the universe; a plethora of committees and opportunities for helping disadvantaged people and preserving the environment; and an open, questioning approach to personal faith as opposed to a blind, unthinking belief in whatever one has been told to believe, be it Catholicism or any religious tradition. The faith of a UU person thus strikes me as more meaningful because it is arrived at, over and over again, through an ever-evolving process of spiritual growth.

For me, being even a nominal part of a UU community means that I know I am a valuable thread in the tapestry of the world, and that my thread is intertwined with every other in a mysterious pattern that will in the end be woven for the good. It means that I can be assured that others in the community will help me meet my needs—and that I will likewise help others meet theirs. And that all of us will tolerate, nay, celebrate each other's differences—otherwise the tapestry would be only one hue and pattern, instead of the complexity of many.

I also have my own special form of prayer, which I developed at the age of 16 while in my junior year of high school (as it happens, the year before the all-consuming first depression). I remember that I was sick with a respiratory infection, and so was excused from a physics test right before it began, to go to the infirmary. Once there, the idea somehow came into my head to pray for four of my close friends who were in the classroom taking this test. Except this time I didn't just say, "Dear God, please give my friends an A on the physics test," the way I would have ordinarily.

Instead, a sudden intuition led me to separately imagine each of the four girls, placing each in my mind's eye in the palm of God's hand, surrounded by gentle colored light. I summoned up an image of the girls, one at a time, in a spring meadow with flowers and trees growing and a shining sky, in vibrant colors. This kind of "praying" was done without words, and seemed perfectly natural to me as someone profoundly affected by colors and images, someone with a very visual imagination.

I might have forgotten about the prayers, except for the physics teacher's announcement a couple of days later that four people in the class had gotten perfect 100s on the test: they turned out to be the four friends I'd prayed for. Now I knew that this kind of prayer really worked. And I didn't feel that I was so great, making things happen for the people I'd prayed for. It seemed instead that I had merely been a vessel through which the power of God had flowed.

Since that instance, I've always turned to this praying-in-images whenever a particularly important decision looms, or a loved one finds herself or himself in a difficult situation. This method always seems to bring about a fruitful resolution to the problem. I also say silently, "God, be with me [or us]" whenever I'm in need, especially when I'm very anxious. She always brings peace, and a sense that everything will be all right.

American writer Richard Bach wrote: "The best way to pay for a beautiful moment is to enjoy it." All of the wonderful people and events in my life—and they do exist, despite the gray-colored glasses I've worn during depressions—I fear their loss so much that I'm always waiting for the other shoe to drop. It's so easy for me to preoccupy myself with all the horrible things that are just waiting to happen, at any unpredictable time (having internalized the way I did so in childhood), that I lose sight of the beautiful moments that may be happening right now.

That's where God is—in those lovely people and moments. Not in the tragedies around the corner. I'm starting to see now that it doesn't make sense to fear the future at the expense of the present. Nor does it make sense to believe God is punishing me for my sins; maybe She is actually easing my past suffering by sending me the magnificent evidence of Her love.

True, eventually bad things will happen to me, but bad things are woven into everyone's tapestry. Yes, Tom will die; my parents and brothers and sisters will die; before that my beloved cat will die; menopause may deal me particularly harsh blows as the end of my potential child-bearing days loom; or we could lose our house or our jobs. But I think, with the sustenance of God and everyone in our lives, we will be able to handle what life gives us. Sometimes I can only hope that Tom and I will be equal to whatever challenges come; sometimes I have doubts about my own strength. But probably everyone, not just people with bipolar disorder, has these doubts.

On the other hand, sometimes I'm not doing so well, and my feelings and thoughts flow in another direction. If I'm depressed, sometimes the suicidal ideation returns and I wonder if it might not be preferable to die now, while I have lots of good memories, before all the Bad Future Things can happen to me. I haven't seriously planned for suicide in years, but I have felt very fleetingly suicidal, even in the recent years I've been with Tom. And it hasn't been because of him or my life circumstances, but despite them. I don't think I'm very close to God at those moments.

Sometimes I wake up in the morning and just don't want to do anything that day: not go to work, not clean up the house, and not even get out of bed. That's not necessarily depression; I think everyone feels like that sometimes. But at those times my baseline energy level seems lower than that of a lot of people I know—which apparently is true for many people with bipolar disorder on such days.

For example, I went through two stints in grad school with women who held down full-time jobs *and* went to school full-time—whereas often I worked my NIMH job part-time while I was in school, did my practicum experience part-time, and attended classes part-time. And I was frequently exhausted and depressed while doing so. Not to mention that I never joined these young women in socializing on weekends once their schoolwork was done—I was too busy sleeping or attempting to study.

Even when I'm in a state of mania, it tends to be dysphoric mania. In those cases, I have energy, yes, but it's the energy of desperate tension that discharges itself in pacing or hand-wringing or even weeping in frustration. I can't seem to reach any relief from the internal engine that drives me, not to focused action but more often to wretched rumination and worry. My thoughts whiz past too quickly to pin down, slamming discordantly like the hammers of piano keys onto my brain and disturbing my peace.

I'm actually more likely to crave suicide as a reprieve from the clamor in mania than from milder depressions. At such times, I'm apt to veer toward paranoia, believing that everyone hates me and is laughing and talking about me. I can't escape all that negative judgment, so why not put an end to the malice I "know" they all hold toward me by putting an end to myself?

In 2003, shortly before Tom and I were married, I participated in a genetic/diagnostic study of bipolar disorder at Johns Hopkins University. I remember conversing with Dean MacKinnon, M.D., an accomplished and empathic psychiatrist, about my rapid mood cycles and struggles with present anxiety, past suicidality, and simply finding a place in the "normal" world.

Since that time, Dr. MacKinnon and his colleagues have published a number of papers in journals like the *American Journal of Psychiatry* and *Bipolar Disorders* concerning the emerging results of their research. I've read as many of these reports as I could, and have found that MacKinnon et al. believe that suicidal tendencies may be more prevalent among rapid cyclers, particularly those who are impulsive while in tumultuous mixed states (of which I've experienced many).

I think these researchers are right on the money. Personally, I've found that when I'm in the turmoil of a mixed state, I feel frantically pushed first in one direction and then in another. It's so easy and so compelling to do something impulsive just to escape all that adrenaline and anxiety. Fortunately, after years of experience with these mood states, I've stopped cutting myself and started painting, or talking, or even pacing—all much better methods of expending that terrible energy. But the temptation to do something self-destructive sometimes still lurks in the shadows at those times.

I know this struggle is one almost every person who endures a mood disorder wrestles with at some point. It just might be God or the greater force-for-good in the universe that saves me at such moments, that pulls me away from death and back toward life. I don't know that I'm always equal to the task all by myself. Moods are powerful, but She is more powerful.

God's healing and the spiritual reawakening it brought and still brings, I am convinced, is one of the most important keys to retaining my well-being and sense of being right with the world, the universe. My Higher Power has brought me hope, and She (I do tend to think of God in feminine terms, as a Sister or Friend who is always with me) leads me toward the wholeness that is so essential to guiding other people in their journey toward being whole.

ART THERAPY AND BEYOND

I've witnessed the power of the holistic healing I wish modern medicine would incorporate, both in my own life and in others' through creative writing and, most especially, through expressive art. During my first hospitalization I discovered art therapy and, guided by an empathic art therapist, for the first time let my throttled-up feelings flow through my brush. After I experienced the catharsis of my first abstract acrylic painting, the art therapist commented, "I see a lot of anger in your picture." And I suddenly realized how insightful she was: I had indeed spattered a messy surfeit of gloppy red, black, and acid green paint onto the canvas in an outpouring of rage. How imPerfect of me! But, I saw (literally!), how real, and how human.

Years before my first exposure to art therapy in the psychiatric hospital in 1984, I loved to look at and create art. From the age of four or five, a crayon was always in my hand. Throughout childhood and adolescence I could amuse myself for hours on end by drawing people and abstract designs. One of my favorite games in middle school involved picking three crayons at random from a box of 64 (one of my most loved possessions) and then drawing clothing ensembles for a female model I had inked, using only those colors.

Color, in fact, has always been the primary facet of art for me—I am first absorbed by the provocative emotional power of color in my own and others' art, before line and form. At the age of five I remember drawing a portrait of myself, a Caucasian person, and using for my flesh tone an orange crayon, rather than the pink one my classmates of the same ethnicity were using. My kindergarten teacher asked why I hadn't used pink, but I insisted that my skin was closer to orange than pink. Regardless of which of us was "right," I had strong opinions about color even then.

As I grew older and started experiencing sharp mood swings, my color choices both influenced and were influenced by my moods. When depressed or euthymic, I preferred cool blues, greens, and dark hues, while I only dared to wear red, yellow, and orange if hypomanic. For me, failure to match clothing colors harmoniously was and is a sign of emotional disequilibrium.

As well, I've always had an intense visual imagination. Merely glancing at a grotesque book illustration of a monster as a child—or seeing a few seconds of a gory or disturbing scene in a crime drama or horror film as an adult—has felt intolerable. The offending image would be fixed in my memory for years to come, in both horrific nightmares and lingering memories. On the other hand, I've always been able to remember phone numbers exceptionally well, because I can see them in my mind's eye. I'm also not bad at the supposedly "male" skill of mentally rotating figures in 3D space.

When my next-younger sister Ellen and I were very young, my mother hung two prints in our shared bedroom, both by Renoir: *A Girl With a Watering Can* and *Girl With a Hoop*. She told us that the blonde girl was me and that the brunette girl rolling a hoop was my sister. It was true that the girl with the watering can looked uncannily like me at my age then, about four, so of course I took her word as the solemn truth. Until laughingly corrected by my mom a couple of years later, I marveled at the idea that a famous artist (I didn't know he'd been dead for many decades) could portray me so well. I first resolved then to someday be an artist myself, so I could move other people's emotions as profoundly as this picture had done to me (though of course I didn't conceive of this plan in quite those words at such a young age)!

As I became an adolescent and studied art more formally in high school, I became enamored with the Impressionists, Post-Impressionists, and some of the Abstract Expressionists. I started going to art museums, like the two wings of the National Gallery of Art (its West Building and East Building), the National Museum of Women in the Arts, and the Phillips Collection, where I wandered dreamily through halls hung with my favorites: Renoir (of course), Bonnard, Monet, Cassatt, Rauschenberg, Rothko, Picasso, El Greco, O'Keefe, and van Gogh, the artist dearest to my heart. Van Gogh's moody, swirling landscapes and self-portraits captivated me with their rich, haunting colors and soulful movement.

Later, as my depression deepened, I gazed often at his *Wheatfield With Crows*, executed right before his suicide, and pondered my emotional kinship with him. But the truth was that, in the period right before I received treatment for my depression, my creativity had dwindled to nothing. It was only during my recovery while in the hospital that my creative urges reawakened and I began to paint with a new freedom and fluency. It was then that I abandoned strictly representational art-making and let myself explore the continent of my unconscious through my own style of abstract expressionism.

Since then, I've returned to painting whenever my creative juices have flowed. I've learned, however, that this wellspring cannot be controlled or forced. I just have to let the need to make art take me where it wants to lead, when it wants to lead. This may be just another way of saying I'm not nearly as disciplined as I should be about keeping up with my art. I know that if I were more disciplined and steady, I would produce a lot more than I do. Unfortunately, I tend to get busy with everyday life, and because I'm not a professional artist (and I don't kid myself that I'm good enough to be one), I'm not always as motivated as I could be. But I do try to listen to my inner creative voice—after all, it led me to write this book.

The deepest reason I generate art is to bring peace to myself and others. As I mentioned earlier, painting and writing have helped me pour out emotions that were too passionate to hold inside, giving the feelings a safe container. As Wordsworth said, poetry is "emotion recollected in tranquility." The poems I've written over the years, particularly when upset, may have been sophomoric but at least they have brought me tranquility.

Likewise, the process of brushing paint onto canvas calms and soothes me when I am caught in chaos. And the art and poems or writings don't only serve to help me. I've long been in the habit of writing a poem or painting a picture for a specific friend or family member—a labor of love. In such a situation, I really believe it is "the thought that counts" because, while my gifts may not be objectively great works of art, and though I don't always know that they are appreciated by their recipient, they are shared in the spirit of healing.

I've felt the palliative effects of art in my own life, as I've developed my own style of abstract painting. My husband Tom and I joke about the times I've been vexed with him and, unable to sleep, swooped paint onto canvas with my brush and sometimes even with my fingers in the middle of the night to pour out my frustration in vivid colors. By the following morning, my anger has invariably disappeared yet I've constructed a tangible container for my erstwhile emotional turbulence.

I've also been privileged to witness psychic healing in other people through art therapy. That powerful memory stayed with me long after my first expressive experience in the hospital art studio, and 10 years later guided me to the decision that I ardently wanted to become an art therapist myself. I knew in my fundament that art was at once soothing and empowering for those of us who needed psychic healing. Here was my chance to give back the help that I had once been given: I applied and was accepted to George Washington University master's program in art therapy in 1996.

Soon immersed in class discussions, readings, personal art-making, and practicum experience at various psychiatric hospitals in the Washington, DC, area, I eagerly gave myself up to this new world in which creative transformations continually emerged, in myself and in the lives of the broken people I served. I soon saw the need to resist any solipsistic tendencies I might have regarding my own mental pain or history when I began to meet children, adolescents, and adults young and old who clearly were suffering more than I could ever imagine. I encountered sexually active 11-year-olds; kindergartners who had been abused by their original parents almost to death; parolees struggling to stay sober; men with schizophrenia who never spoke once in art therapy sessions over a year's time spent with them; women with comorbid mood and personality disorders who apprehensively resisted ECT treatment and verbally pushed away therapy group members who intruded too far into their comfort zone.

I facilitated and witnessed these people's artistic creations: all were wondrous, some laden with painted metaphors like the woman with bipolar disorder who often cried during sessions and was able to express the quintessence of her illness in two starkly contrasting images, a large black circle representing the black hole of her depression and a bright red, orange, and gold starburst embodying her mania. Others' art works were muddy watercolors of listlessness and anergia; joyfully simple clay animal playmates; angrily obsessive filled-in-the-lines geometric pencil patterns; mutely elegant wood sculptures. Most of these creations seemed to afford their creators at least a temporary reprieve from the anguish they carried through their lives.

Over the three years I spent in the art therapy program, I met myriad challenges in attempting to help the patients in the hospitals at which I worked. Trying to rein in large groups of children with attention-deficit-hyperactivity disorder left me exasperated and drained. Nor did I appreciate all of the sessions I led with teenagers, some of whom expressed their hostility toward me and toward the suggestion to make art by swinging bags of wet clay at me! I also felt uncomfortable around their teeming hormones and never was able to successfully resolve my unease. After a few such art therapy sessions, I decided that working with adolescents was not my forte. I generally did enjoy facilitating groups with adults, regardless of diagnosis, since they tended to be more insightful about their problems, but I certainly encountered my share of resistance to making art and the resultant self-examination it inevitably engendered. At times I decided to cope with people's reluctance by playing classical or jazz music during the sessions and using guided imagery, or by having a writing group instead, in which, for example, I invited the group participants to write a letter they didn't necessarily have to send, to someone with whom they needed closure over past issues.

In terms of my art therapy program days, although I usually enjoyed the thought-provoking readings for my classes and the resultant class discussions and experiential art-making sessions, I always dreaded weekly group "supervision" night. In this class, we all took turns analyzing therapeutic interventions we had made with clients in the past week, and why we felt we'd succeeded or failed to help them. Our professor and other class members freely joined in the discussion to offer feedback. Due to my persistent insecurity and almost unshakeable feeling that everyone else in the class knew exactly what she or he was doing while I was just bumbling along, revealing my perceived shortcomings as a fledging art therapist unnerved me.

I also remember that, in most new semester's supervision classes, I summoned the courage to reveal to my classmates that I was bipolar. Now I'm not sure why I did that; I suspect I was pathetically offering an excuse for my therapeutic failings. Maybe I was trying to elicit sympathy, or maybe I just wanted attention that wasn't focused on what I could have done better in my interactions with my clients. Whatever my ulterior motive, if I could go back to those grad student days, I don't think I would reveal my illness to anyone except close friends in my classes. However, I think I was justified in telling my professors about my disorder because of the couple of times I needed a reasonable accommodation to finish a paper or project, since during the three years I took classes and the year in which I wrote my thesis, I was depressed much of the time. It was all I could do to manage work, my practicum internship, plus two classes per semester; on weekends I seemed to do nothing more than sleep and study.

Anyway, I mention my disclosure of my illness to my peers and professors because it now seems that this was unnecessary for the most part. Except for periods when I needed extra time to complete a paper due to depression, I should have been focusing on my clients' needs for wholeness, not my own selfish need for attention and, perhaps, sympathy or pity.

Perhaps because of this perceived proclivity for making mistakes, while I do have a graduate degree in art therapy, I only utilized this education as a practicing art therapist for a few years on a very part-time basis. At the time I thought it simply wasn't the most practical of degrees, and though I was not currently practicing art therapy, I was still helping people with severe mental illnesses, albeit in an indirect manner, at NIMH. I'm glad I obtained my art therapy degree, I placated myself, because it led me to a tremendous fund of knowledge and insight about healing people in pain and about my own psyche. No amount of psychotropic medication, no matter how ameliorative, can substitute for the catalyst for wellness that expressive artistic creation affords. Medicine heals the brain, but art heals the soul.

TREAD SOFTLY, FOR YOU TREAD ON MY DREAMS

My art, as a touchstone for my soul, has been rich in color and drama. But the dreams that enfold me in sleep have evoked even more portentous imagery and emotion, capturing my soul through the webs they spin. The "art" in my dreams has often been by turns healing and unsettling.

From early childhood, I've always been able to remember my dreams, which have been extraordinarily vivid. At the age of seven, I woke up sobbing as a dream-character whispered "It was only a dream" after I'd just been surrounded by all the people I loved at a wonderful picnic in an enchanted forest. I tried in vain to pull myself back under, back into the fairy-tale dream, but of course it was too late. This somehow seemed emblematic of my life then: my depression left me craving safety and succor I felt I would never have.

When I was 12 years old, another striking dream found me in a watery moonscape where the sky was teal and I petted an ice-blue kitten with melting eyes named "Moondrop." This dream made such an impression on me that I wrote it down and drew a picture of the kitten, little knowing that one day I would count a white cat with similarly piercing eyes as the bright spot of my day, coming home alone to an apartment empty save for her, as I did for several years before Tom and I moved in together. This cat, now 19 years old, is my dear companion still, and she now enjoys the love of both Tom and me. "Bonkers" (a stigmatizing name, yes, but another family member, not I, was the one who named her!) may not have long left to live, but whenever she meows her last, she will know she was loved long and well.

From puberty and throughout my adolescence, boys on whom I had secret crushes made regular visits in my dreams. Typically, I would be following one of them through a crowded building or across a midnight field, as they perpetually eluded me, usually not even aware I was there.

Again, this seemed to mirror my waking-life situation. Unrequited love was my constant companion as a lonely teenager.

Dreams also have informed my therapy process, as both my psychiatrist and psychotherapist have helped me interpret them with an eye toward relevant issues in my daily life. One that comes to mind is a dream of about eight years ago: I was trying to rescue tomato plants in a garden that had flooded. I submerged my hand in the water and pulled out . . . not a red but a *turquoise* tomato. Somehow while dreaming I knew that this tomato represented me in my uniqueness. I woke up with a rekindled sense of the depths of richness hiding beneath the surface of my psyche, as well as a renewed confidence in my worth, despite having a mental illness. Yes, I was different, but that only helped make me who I was, a one-of-a-kind creation.

I've also been lucky enough to have frequent lucid dreams, which I've cultivated to some degree by training myself to recognize that I'm dreaming, while I'm dreaming. I use techniques such as allowing an object or strange event that tends to recur in my particular dreams to signal me that what I'm now experiencing is, in fact, a dream.

For instance, every time I dream that a tiny airplane is descending through the air, close enough for me to reach up and touch, I instantly recognize that I'm dreaming. If I find myself floating through objects or flying over trees or buildings, that also immediately "wakes me up" just enough to be able to control the direction my dream is taking.

My lucid dreams have been among the most powerful and profound ones that I've experienced. In these oneiric voyages, I've healed unresolved conflicts with people I haven't seen for decades; I've witnessed cosmic visions of the oneness of the universe. I've probed the seamlessness of the fabric of space-time; I've taken part in giddy midair acrobatics. These dreams have seemed like mania-while-sleeping!

As can be imagined, however, other dreams are not nearly so delightful. For every sensual or sacredly uplifting dream, a horrible nightmare counters it. I've experienced many nightmares similar, I imagine, to the way a trauma flashback feels to someone with PTSD. During periods of either agitated depression or dysphoric mania, these dreams populate my troubled sleep almost nightly.

One that has visited me often in recent months involves blistering heat and the remains of a shell-shocked city sometime in the future. I read newspaper headlines about nuclear war while crouching desperately with my family and friends in a deserted building, waiting to die. In another version of the "death dream," I'm hiding in a darkened corner at night, huddled and waiting for a mysterious gunman who will inevitably find me and shoot me dead. Often the gunman actually *does* shoot me, and I feel the bullet penetrate my heart. I fervently pray, "God, I love Tom, I love my family and all my friends, please take me to heaven," and just as my soul begins to leave my body in the dream, I wake up breathlessly.

On occasion I dream that I am the one trying to hurt or kill me. Once I was hanging from a noose fashioned from a scarf in my dream. I stepped away from the chair I dreamed that I stood on, and as the dream scarf tightened around my neck, I woke up. At other times, I dream that I am in a dingy hospital, strapped to a table covered with white sheets, being wheeled to get an MRI (which I abhor, being claustrophobic) or ECT (which I would fear). Before my hands are tied down, I try to cut my wrist with a knife; or I try to wrest myself off the gurney to bang my head on the corridor wall. Right after I attempt to hurt myself in the dream, I awaken.

The types of dreams I've just mentioned trouble me far more than those in which I am a passive victim of harm or murder. As I've said, I want never to hurt myself again, let alone commit suicide. These dreams frighten me with the idea that they could be precognitive—that I will in fact do harm to myself at some point in the future. Or, more likely and more menacingly, they could signify that I have strong, heretofore unconscious desires to hurt myself. This would mean that my talk about having moved beyond using self-destructive actions as a solution to emotional discomfort is just that: talk. I have the feeling that I'm dealing with major cognitive dissonance here, to put it mildly.

Musing over these dreams in more depth, however, I've come to the conclusion that they are not so much a harbinger of self-injurious urges or actual self-injury, as warnings from my unconscious to beware such urges. In other words, I must be on guard against tendencies to hurt myself, knowing that they may arise again—but I *can* successfully resist them. With my strong support system of Tom, my parents and brothers and sisters, psychiatrist and psychotherapist, and friends, as well as my own will to keep myself, my harmful behavior truly can be a thing of the past. I certainly do have a dark side, but I believe that my light side, bolstered by the universal force for good I believe lives in me, is stronger and will win in the end.

WEDDED

My "light side" was undoubtedly in ascendance the day my husband and I were married. At last the dream of love I had entertained since adolescence was being fulfilled—not in the frilly, fairy-tale ruffles of reverie, but in the reality of adult love and loyalty.

The years leading up to my wedding belied the fact that one day I would find a person with whom I could share my soul in truth and trust, yet still feel comfortable enough around to burp, or wake up next to with a bad hair day!

Although I successfully stayed away from alcohol and drugs in high school and college, I still had normal sexual urges. I was a teenager, after all, with hormones zipping around and awakening new, sometimes frightening feelings. These emotions terrified me because I worried I'd end up as had a couple of girls I knew: pregnant out of wedlock.

When I'd been 11, and again at 15, two of the older girls in the neighborhood had become pregnant shortly before they were to graduate from high school. These were the 1970s and early '80s, and as a sign of the times, I remember my mom and dad sitting all of us kids down who were in the teen or pre-teen age range, for stern lectures about the dangers of premarital sex. I internalized these lessons swiftly. These unsettling incidents convinced me that I should stay as far away from sex as possible, for as long as possible.

Meanwhile, I held fast to idealized, overly romantic notions about how Love should proceed whenever (if ever) the time came that I did start dating. It was my firm belief that I should not even kiss someone, let alone date him seriously, unless I was completely in love with him and absolutely planned to marry him. And of course I would never do more with a boy than kiss him, because that would be a grave sin.

I berated myself often in my high school and college years for sexual yearnings that I wasn't sure I could control. However, since another human being was almost never actually in the picture, I was for the most part able to comply with my internalized rules about no premarital contact other than kissing—and obviously no sex.

My aforementioned first boyfriend, who gave me my first real kiss, probably liked me well enough. I, on the other hand, was desperately in love with him and idolized him as the love of my life. That he was heretofore the *only* "love of my life" didn't suggest to my addled heart and mind that maybe I wouldn't really marry him and live happily ever after. It simply never occurred to me that the story doesn't necessarily end with your first boyfriend. After we went our separate ways at the end of my Georgetown era, I was heartbroken and angry at being rejected. But I convinced myself that instead I was a trifle relieved, because I no longer had to deal with the troubling physical urges he had awakened in me. Meanwhile, I suspect he was more than a little relieved not to have to deal with my intensity and neediness anymore.

I don't know what ages my more normal brothers and sisters, none of whom have remotely the rigid superego that I do (all the better for them!), first had sex. For me, however, the moment didn't arrive until a few weeks before my 33rd birthday, and the experience was not a pleasant or spiritually exalting one. It hurt—a lot. And I wasn't even sure in my heart of hearts whether I loved the man I was with, though we were in a serious relationship. Immediately afterward, I rebuked myself for not having waited until I got married. The fact that my mom and dad had been relative kids at the ages of their marriage—20 and 22, respectively—didn't mitigate my offense.

After that relationship broke up, several months later, I started going out with my (now) husband, Tom, who was to become the best and last person I would date. I knew I was with the person I was meant to be with—and I know it today. He also cured me of my Puritanism for the most part and injected some much-needed humor into my life.

By doing so, Tom helped me grow up the rest of the way socially. I've found it to be true in my own life, and often in those of friends with psychiatric illnesses, that we tend to have difficulty relating to others appropriately. I think this is because conditions like bipolar disorder and schizophrenia strike us down when we are at the crossroads between childhood and adulthood and impede us from learning the social signals other young people assimilate intuitively.

For instance, I find that I constantly seek other people's approval; I feel that I have to live up to everyone's expectations, even if they conflict with each other. It can seem as though my identity is swallowed up by my engulfing need to be loved by everyone all of the time. No wonder this creates anxiety . . . It's an impossible quest. Yet it seems to be hard-wired in me. I've recently begun working with my psychotherapist again on this, one of the major issues that we tackle; it was also one of the main things I worked on with my psychiatrist's help. I need to find my true self and reclaim it. I hate being so wishy-washy; after all, I do have some strong opinions and drives of my own, and I shouldn't be afraid to express them even in the face of other people's disapproval.

My problem in making decisions is that, in my hunger for approval, I ask the opinion of all those significant to me whenever a choice hangs over my head. This includes everything from what length to cut my hair, to which insurance plan to subscribe to, to whether to obtain further graduate education. And I too often tend to assimilate another person's opinions completely, convincing myself that her or his thoughts on the matter are "the right thing to do"—only to internalize the next person's entirely opposite outlook and reverse my decision.

However, in all the truly important decisions of my life, I have followed my intuitions—which, believe it or not, are strong and clear when it really matters. I knew after my first episode of depression in 1984 that my life's focus was to help other people with mental illness instead of to pursue a career in the performing arts. I knew that my art and writing would save me from despair and dysphoria, and ultimately would lead me to the form my career in the mental health field would take.

And I knew that Tom was finally the man for me, even when I first met him. I know, too, that I was right to listen to the inner voice of my intuition in these decisions. And in knowing Tom, I've been brought from awkward, emotional near-adolescence into womanly maturity as my relationship with him deepened and flourished, leading eventually to marriage.

A verse from Emily Dickinson's poem "Wedded" describes my feelings about my wedding to Tom and subsequent marriage:

> A solemn thing—it was—I said—
> A woman—white—to be—
> And wear—if God should count me fit—
> Her hallowed mystery—

I've been living the mystery that is marriage with Tom for the past seven and one half years, and have loved him for nearly the past ten. I still remember the day we met, April 19, 2001; our wedding was two years to the day later, on April 19, 2003.

That 19th day in April of 2001, Tom was an attendee at a conference on facilitating support groups that two friends from NAMI and I were leading. At the time, I was actually dating someone else. This relationship was waning, but I was trying to convince myself to salvage it, reasoning that I might have no other chances at happiness.

At the conference in Baltimore, MD, I was immediately struck by Tom's friendliness and humor, not to mention deep intelligence. Much to my chagrin, I found myself attracted to him, even more attracted than I was to the person I was supposedly dating. Needless to say, I tried mightily to suppress this feeling.

However, throughout the three-day conference, I found myself talking and laughing with Tom again and again. He was so fascinating and so easy to talk to. When I ran a small group one day to assess how the conference participants were learning the support group model, I was taken by how naturally Tom seemed to fit the role of group facilitator. He also accompanied me on a trip with other conference attendees to the grave of Edgar Allan Poe—and Tom had to squish into the open trunk because we had so many people in one car!

While in downtown Baltimore, our group visited a gay nightclub where a drag show contest was being held. I'd never been in such an exotic place, but I enjoyed myself nevertheless, bantering with Tom over Diet Cokes. On the way back to the hotel, we shared a cab because he had wanted to show me around his native city after the others had left. The cabbie got lost and our cab ride ended up costing $30. I paid the fare, and Tom promised to send me a check for his half if I would give him my address. We parted at the end of the conference with Tom's jokingly urging me to learn to drive (was he prescient?) and a reiteration of his vow to send me a check.

People always say this, but it is true: by the end of that conference, I had an intuition that I would break up with my current boyfriend, get together with Tom, and possibly even marry him eventually. I had never been so drawn to a person in my entire life, and I waited anxiously for any follow-up contact from him.

The promised check did come in a week or so, along with a lengthy and philosophical letter that (of course) I still have. I promptly wrote Tom back, and a beautiful friendship—and that's all it was at first—began. Eventually we realized that our communication would occur more easily through email, and after that a steady flow of emails burned up our computer screens.

About a month after we started emailing, Tom invited me to visit a museum in DC with him on a weekend ("with permission from your beau," he wrote charmingly). I went with him, and we had a wonderful time walking around the National Mall and talking, talking, talking about anything and everything. Tom never made a pass at me, or acted improperly, but I suspected he might be attracted to me anyway, just as I was to him. After he left to make the drive back to Baltimore, I was stunned by the depth of my reaction to him: I felt as though I simply couldn't get enough of him and his warm presence. This despite the fact that we had never even touched.

Over the next few months, we met several other times to peruse museums, and to attend the NAMI conference, which was in Washington, DC, that year. Tom and I never ran out of things to say to one another, and we enjoyed each other's company immensely. We were able to share our stories about our mood disorders—Tom is bipolar, like me. I was able to accept without judgment his accounts of the negative consequences of his manias in his past, as he accepted my recounting of my past self-mutilation and suicidality.

During the NAMI convention, I called my erstwhile boyfriend to tell him I felt it best that we stop seeing each other, and he took the news agreeably. Perhaps he had realized that the relationship was no longer on firm footing, if it earlier had been. The next day I told Tom what I had done and invited him to a party at the home of one of my sisters who lived in the area.

Although I had described Tom at length to my local brothers and sisters, who were all for my dating him if the opportunity arose, I felt anxious the evening of the party about my sister's reaction to him. It was very important to me for my family to approve of Tom. But I needn't have worried; all of my brothers and sisters who were at the party liked him very much (though not as much as I did)!

After that, we finally began dating; our first "official" date was the next weekend, when Tom took me to my first-ever Orioles game. Though I'm not a baseball fan, and was not thrilled by the 100+ degree heat that afternoon, all that mattered was that I was sitting next to Tom. That evening we kissed for the first time; I flew home on wings of rhapsody.

We quickly settled into a routine of seeing each other each weekend (since at that point I lived in Arlington, VA, and he lived in Baltimore, MD, about 50 miles to the northeast), and we soon met the rest of each other's families. Tom attended my brother's wedding with me, and effortlessly fit in with my quirky family, as I grew to like his parents and brothers, one of whom had a family of his own. Around the Thanksgiving holidays, we moved in together to my Arlington apartment, and the relationship became more serious.

Tom and I started talking about marriage, though we didn't have a timeframe as yet and didn't want to rush into it prematurely. It did seem the natural next step to us, because we had transitioned smoothly from seeing each other on weekends to living together, and both of us had never been so happy. For me, being with Tom marked the first time I had been in a romantic relationship in which I truly felt loved by the other person. And I knew that I loved him with a profundity and joy I had never felt before with anyone else. We simply belonged together, and belonged to each other.

Tom proposed to me on March 8, 2002, and I proudly wore the ring he gave me for the next year as we planned our wedding. Thankfully, we were able to secure the Sculpture Garden of the American Visionary Art Museum for April 19, 2003, as the location for our wedding ceremony and reception. The Visionary Art Museum, situated in Baltimore's Inner Harbor near Federal Hill, is home to the marvelous, funky, and absolutely unique art of self-taught "visionary" artists, many of whom have grappled with mental illness and found self-expression through creativity even while institutionalized. We had discovered this museum shortly after we started dating, and it suited both our personalities and our love for making and viewing art. We couldn't conceive of a more fitting place for our wedding.

Although I occasionally had had bouts of anxiety in the months leading up to our wedding, usually brought on by the logistics of planning it, as the morning of April 19, 2003, dawned, I felt only joy and anticipation of the joining of Tom's and my hearts and lives. A non-denominational female minister performed the ceremony we had written ourselves, which included a handfasting (a traditional Celtic ceremony involving the binding of our crossed and joined hands together with a special ribbon we had chosen), presenting roses to our mothers, and my sisters singing "The Prayer of St. Francis" and proclaiming a Scripture reading. I had never felt so close to Tom, and friends afterwards told me that we had both "glowed" during the ceremony.

People had warned me that "after the wedding, real life sets in," a life that could be dull and burdensome. But, at least speaking for myself, that hasn't been the case. Of course, Tom and I soon ensconced ourselves in the daily routine of going to work, cleaning house, fixing dinner, paying bills. And of course at times we've had disagreements and miscommunications.

But we've learned, and continue to learn, to talk things out rather than suffer in silence. To give each other honest feedback if one of us appears symptomatic or unhappy. To support each other through difficult times. Tom has helped me through two unsuccessful medication changes and an ER visit for seeming heart problems (in actuality, an anxiety attack). And I've supported him through several months of unemployment after he finished a graduate certificate and couldn't immediately find work. No matter how we might get on each other's nerves occasionally, both of us know we have the other's love and that we're not going to call it quits.

Although the circumstance of us both being bipolar would likely be a hindrance on many levels to our having a child, and many would argue that it could only breed instability, we have actually found our mutual bipolarity to be a comfort most of the time. Because Tom and I are so familiar with all the warning signs and symptoms, the loneliness and desperation of depression and the seductive highs of mania, each of us understands the other on a more innately meaningful level than "ordinary" married couples might. At least that's what we think.

And each of us is so sensitive to the merest hint of a dip or rise in mood in the other and can immediately point out our observation. For instance, Tom intercedes right away if I impulsively speak of an urge to bang my head in frustration (even though we both know I won't actually do it) or if I even appear more sad than usual. And I rush to let him know if it seems that he's been making impulse purchases that could lead to spending beyond our means; on the other hand, if his confidence level seems low, I try to help him raise it.

Of course, there are all sorts of benefits to marriage in general, and to being with Tom in particular, that have nothing to do with bipolarity or the lack thereof. Tom and I have lots of silly, private nicknames and phrases that make us laugh. In public, one of us will quickly wink at the other with a secret smile, prompting a wink and smile back—meaning "I love you."

No matter how worried I get over some problem I can't do anything about, Tom never fails to laugh me out of my dour mood. As I've been writing this book, he's consistently encouraged me and nourished my urge to write. Tom even came up with some of the themes and structures underlying the book, such as the narratives from important people in my life that I've interspersed with my own words.

By the same token, Tom has told me that, until he met me, he had only dabbled in making art. Now, he says, through benefit of my encouragement and my own love for art, he has discovered in himself a great fascination for creating patterns with geometrical shapes and color, and he is in the midst of crafting a "triangle series," as well as exploring nature photography with his digital camera. He has a gift for capturing fleeting moments of birds in flight or butterflies alighting on my niece's dress in a garden.

One of the crucial things I've had to learn in marriage to Tom is controlling my need to control. With the help of my psychotherapist, I've discovered that I do have a strong urge to control everything that happens to me and the way people react to me, purely out of fear of the unknown and of rejection. This translates, in my interactions with Tom, into too much encouragement—what could be considered pushing, to call a spade a spade—in directions he may not want or need to go.

Tom has a long history of work as a toxicologist for a major laboratory, which ended about a year before he met me. Since then, he's reinvented himself in several ways career-wise: he's worked in a drop-in center for homeless people with mental illness; on a research contract in my branch (adult schizophrenia genetics) at NIMH; and now, at a highly regarded health research nonprofit firm as an information specialist. As you can see, the constant has been his love of science and health, especially mental health.

But lately, as I've looked from time to time for alternate jobs for myself, imagining what it would be like to work outside of NIMH, I've fastened on to science and lab opportunities that have looked promising (read: profitable) for Tom when I came across them. Then I would approach Tom, enthusiastic about great lab jobs at which I thought he'd excel, and urge him to apply for these jobs, only to meet his lack of enthusiasm. For quite a while, I secretly wondered, "What's wrong with him that he doesn't want to apply for this wonderful, high-paying job?"

Only recently have I realized that the question I should have been asking instead is "What's wrong with me that I'm pushing him to apply for jobs he doesn't want?" I've finally begun to let Tom take his own path, just as he has always encouraged me to take mine. He came up with a plan to continue working at his health research firm, aspiring to a research assistant position after taking classes in research methods and statistics as the research experts at the company have advised him to do. No, he won't instantly make more money, but he will gain something much more important: job satisfaction, with the knowledge that he followed his heart.

Sometimes I wonder how Tom put up with my interfering with his work life all those months. I guess he loves me. Now I have to love him enough to let him do things his own way.

And our mutual love is a most powerful healing force. My mother and father helped me immensely with their love, support, and refusal to stop believing in me and my potential to be whatever I wanted to be, back when I was a frightened teenager emerging from her first episode, and beyond through my young adulthood. In my life now, it is Tom who is my family, who helps keep me well as my parents did then. The only way for me to repay Tom for lovingly helping me bear my burdens is to help him bear his. In fact, we carry each other, and always will. Our hearts and souls are joined by a connection that began when our hands were bound together in our marriage ceremony.

CHOICES AND CHILDREN

When adults asked me "what I wanted to be when I grew up," the five-year-old me whose boundaries between herself and her mother were still blurred declared that "I want to be a mommy"—nothing more. At the age of 10, I wanted to be an artist, a teacher, an archaeologist, a singer, an actress, a scientist, a doctor, a novelist—but still, of course, a mother. In adolescence and young adulthood, as I overcame my early episodes of depression and mania and began to believe that maybe I actually would be able to marry someday, I never doubted that I would have children. After all, as one of a sibship of 12, being surrounded by kids seemed natural and right—even if I didn't feel entirely comfortable around babies and wasn't looking forward to the supposed agony of pregnancy and childbirth.

But, as it happened, I did indeed get married, and my biological baby clock began sounding its alarm around age 38 or 39—right on schedule. Sometimes I would even dream that I was pregnant. One or two such dreams I was able to dismiss, but soon I was dreaming about having my own child—more often than not a baby girl—on the order of one or two times a week.

During those days, Tom and I visited a hospital to see a work friend's new, precious, baby boy. I marveled at this young miraculous life, almost afraid to gingerly touch his tiny down-covered head as he gazed at me with wondering, wide eyes. Of course I had the dream that night. I was pregnant with a girl who would have curly blonde hair and blue eyes, like I had at birth, and like Tom too sported in his baby pictures.

Several days later, when my period hadn't come on the day it always does, I wondered . . . hoping and fearing. Then the next day, it arrived and I sighed, both in disappointment and in relief. But at the time I believed that having a family would probably never work for me, for us. Not having children was the decision my husband and I would probably end up making, however regretfully, I told myself. I convinced myself I was glad that at least we saw eye-to-eye on this choice . . . even though I sensed that we both inwardly might wish things were different.

Those dreams and images and desires continued to haunt me, though, so that I continued to talk about the possibility more with Tom, and with my psychotherapist, as well as with my sisters and brother who have children. I didn't feel that I should dismiss out of hand the idea of having a daughter or son of my own.

My sister, who has three creative, sweet boys, cautioned me that, naturally, having children requires a total lifestyle change, and that once it's done it can't be undone. In other words, she said, don't have kids if you're still ambivalent about it. But I told her that when I was younger I always did want to have children; I just gave that up as a pipe-dream once I got sick. Now, I told her, I wasn't really sick anymore . . . so maybe Tom and I really could have a child. I said I was aware that I'd have to be carefully monitored while I was pregnant so that I could stop taking any teratogenic medications like Depakote, and instead could go on safer ones, or have ECT if necessary—all under my psychiatrist's care.

My sister has been able to stay at home with her three little boys for the most part, and I thought that if I had a child, I'd want to stay home with him or her too. As my sister said, she didn't want to miss the important moments with them—a baby's first steps, first words, precious things like that.

I knew that if Tom and I did have a child, I'd have to put on hold my career plans for going back to school and for whatever else the mental health field might offer me or I could offer the field. I told my psychotherapist that maybe I didn't have the gift of being able to be a mother, that maybe I'd have to settle—though that's not really the right word—for helping people to whom I wasn't related, for using my talents that way. But why couldn't I do both?

If Tom and I had our own children, could we assume that most vital work of tending the bloom of their young lives, of helping them and watching them grow up to be all they could be? My psychotherapist told me that this wish of mine represented noted psychologist Erik Erikson's posited human desire for generativity, for the ultimate act of creativity: to sow in our own child, as I expressed it, the seeds of the most wonderful traits found in my husband and in me.

I wrote earlier about my "gifts of love and creativity," the paintings and poems I've crafted and then given to my loved ones. I explained to my psychotherapist that having a son or daughter with Tom would be the highest gift of love possible—and the love would be shared among all three of us, and with God too. I wasn't necessarily speaking of God in an orthodox religious sense, but of the sharing of the creative positive force in which the whole universe participates—that is kindled in each new birth. I knew I was waxing somewhat rhapsodic, but I had been doing a lot of musing about having children, and I believed it could be the most wondrous thing two people can do together.

Of course, I've always been more idealistic than realistic—maybe I wouldn't sound so rhapsodic in the muddle of soiled diapers and baby's cries and lost sleep and crimped budgets. Even in a perfect world, I'd still have to listen to and attempt to quiet the fussiness of colic; to awaken in the middle of the night to heat up bottles of formula; to change foul-smelling, messy diapers that would wrinkle my sensitive nose.

I know it doesn't stop with infancy, either. When I do daydream about babies, I dwell fearfully on the years and years (18 at least) of actually raising another human being. How would I know how to give my child both the freedom and permission to be creative, and the discipline and boundaries to be safe and responsible? How would I, the consummate worrier, learn how to just let my anxiety ride as my child learned to walk; to ride a bike; to go to school and socialize and study; to date; to drive; finally, to leave?

But, I figured, how would we know except by finding out for ourselves? By entering into the great adventure that so many people journey through, and have since time began? As I told my psychotherapist, I was beginning to realize that I shouldn't count myself out of this most basic and beautiful of human experiences just because I have bipolar disorder. (And who knows, maybe I'd learn to drive someday too! If I were going to have a daughter or son to take to school and activities and friends' homes, I guess I'd have to know how . . .) In the words of a well-known quote by writer Richard Bach: "Argue for your limitations, and sure enough, they're yours." If I believed strongly enough that I was too ineffectual to raise a child, and too scared to cross a highway, and too hypervigilant to drive a car—well, perhaps these would become self-fulfilling prophecies.

And many of my greatest successes, as I discussed with my psychotherapist, I achieved by refusing to believe I couldn't do something. I never thought I couldn't attend college; it didn't occur to me that I wouldn't be able to hold down a full-time job or go to graduate school; once I met Tom, I knew I could succeed at a strong marriage. I've been correct on all counts.

Besides, as Reverend Alberta Eaton reminded us in the sermon she gave at our wedding, we don't have to do anything alone. Not only can we lean on each other, but also we both have families and friends near us who love us and will help us—with staying afloat on the bipolar current, with emotional support, maybe even with raising a daughter or son. Especially since I believe it really does, to quote Hillary Clinton (herself a strong mother of a young woman), "take a village" to bring up a child.

Within the months after my initial soul-searching about having children, I met four babies and small children in my social activities. One weekend I went to a women's spiritual gathering, where two of the women had little children. It was enchanting to watch them play together, but it wasn't enchanting to hear them scream when they got tired. The next day, Tom and I went to a party at a friend's house and encountered a nine-month-old boy and a year-old girl. I was captivated by the baby boy with big brown eyes and a delightful laugh, half-Vietnamese and half-Russian. The little girl had just learned to walk—and she knocked over glasses of juice and soda repeatedly. They each were clearly their own person.

At the spiritual meeting, I spoke to the women present about my intent to pray about the decision whether to have a child. And I continued to do so, with no clear results. However, for whatever reason, since that meeting I stopped having those dreams in which I was pregnant. Many of the women at that spiritual gathering, mothers themselves, had seemed to endorse motherhood; one person laughingly said she thought I'd come back to next year's meeting pregnant. At the time, I secretly wished that could be true—later that day I broke down crying while talking to Tom about it, when he expressed some very reasonable doubts.

But he was right in his doubts—namely, that the unavoidable lack of sleep that having a young baby brings would severely disrupt both of our sleep-wake cycles. Not a desirable thing for two people with bipolar disorder. He also said—and of course, I've mentioned this before and I agree with him—that he wouldn't wish bipolar disorder or depression on anyone, and there is a good chance a child of ours would be afflicted with a mood disorder. Also, according to the genetic law of anticipation, offspring tend to have an earlier onset of an inherited disease than their parents; both of us first sunk into depression in childhood, so how young would a son or daughter of ours get the disease? True, medical science may well come up with a wonderful breakthrough that cures or very effectively treats depression and bipolar disorder by the time our child or children were to grow up, but I'm not sure I want to take that risk.

This helped me realize that if Tom and I did decide to have a child—and probably one would have been all we could handle—we would have to do it for the right reasons. Because we really wanted to bring forth new life into the world and nurture our child—not because I wanted to keep up with my fertile brothers and sisters; or so I wouldn't disappoint my parents and in-laws who may want another grandchild; or to prove to myself, my family, my doctors, or the rest of the world that I could be "normal."

And even in my early 30s, I began to realize how much of a toll my illness had taken and would continue to take on me—if only in the domain of child-raising. I was, and am, highly functional the vast majority of the time, but I know my limitations. I doubted, and still doubt, my ability to handle this most awesome and sober of tasks: that of raising another human being.

Not only do I consider myself bereft of the cool head and unflappable judgment required to take care of a child in the best of times. In the worst of times, another severe episode would render me incapable of caring for him or her at all, and would likely damage my child emotionally and cognitively. I've read about the deleterious effects of a parent's depression and mania (not to mention psychosis) on a vulnerable child, and would feel terrible about inflicting those effects on my own kin. What I mentioned above about my possible inability to care for my children should I become sick again is doubled with both of us having mood disorders. Thus far Tom and I have been lucky in that only one of us has been manic or depressed at one time, but who can predict the future? It simply seems like too chaotic an atmosphere in which to raise children.

I would hate to have a daughter or son and then find that Tom and I couldn't raise her or him because we destabilized due to the stress or sleep loss of child rearing. I also would dread having a child and subsequently having an episode of severe postpartum depression, or even postpartum psychosis, as did my grandmother. Knowing my genetic risk ahead of time, how could I bring a child into the world, only to damage her or him because I couldn't properly take care of her or him? Maybe I'm just crafting excuses to avoid doing something arduous, but I am scared stiff of this undertaking. I do believe that some people shouldn't be mothers, and I may be one of them.

To sum up the problem, a double-whammy bipolar family history (both sides of my and my husband's families), not to mention the deep conviction that I could never be an adequate parent (it takes all my effort to keep myself together!), along with my and my husband's ever-advancing age and an inadequate income to care for a child plus the two of us, all seal the deal. The answer, sadly, divine or profane, seemed to be no.

But I did not want to take no for an answer. I consulted with my psychiatrist and my gynecologist, both of whom I asked for advice concerning the matter of child-bearing. My psychiatrist told me he wouldn't advise me to become pregnant, and that it might be much easier on the child as well as on Tom and me if we adopted instead. That way I wouldn't have to be off my medication, in light of the fact that I'm "exquisitely sensitive" (my doctor's term) to its effects and to the effects of going off it.

My gynecologist was even more emphatic that pregnancy was probably not in the cards for me. She told me that I'd most likely have to be without meds for over a year, maybe a year and nine months: it could take a year for a (then) 39-year-old woman to get pregnant, plus the pregnancy itself. And I knew I'd deteriorate into a total basket case without meds for that long. After all, I become emotionally labile and slightly paranoid if I forget to take a single dose!

Again, she stressed adoption, particularly adoption of a child who was two to three years old. In that case, I wouldn't have my sleep cycle disrupted as much as with a newborn, and Tom and I would avoid passing on our mood genes at the same time. And, fortunately, upon consideration I discovered that I would be as willing to love a child I'd adopted as one that I'd given birth to.

For a while Tom and I seriously considered this option. At the time, neither Tom nor I had any preference about the child's ethnicity; my only stipulation was that I'd rather raise a girl than a boy. But she wouldn't necessarily have to look like Tom and me. I imagined a little girl with almond eyes, dark skin and long, straight, black hair rather than the blonde, curly haired, blue-eyed infant of my previous dreams. And it came to pass that I had a niece, whom her father, my brother, asked me to be the godmother for, who had the blue eyes and blond hair of my toddlerhood and who looked uncannily like I had at that age—which softened the blow of realizing I wouldn't be having a biological daughter.

Friends and family cautioned us, however, that it might be quite difficult to adopt a child, given that we'd be two parents on the older side, with the added complication of both having mental disorders. An adoption agency, looking at two sets of prospective parents, one younger and mentally healthy, and the other one Tom and I, could hardly be blamed for choosing the former rather than choosing us.

Anyway, I'm not perfect and neither is Tom. Our house is quite often messy (unless company is coming over), and laundry, dishes, and other cleaning tasks tend to pile up. Maybe that happens to all families, I don't know; but my point is that, as Tom says sometimes, if we can barely take care of ourselves now, could we really take care of a kid too? Maybe we could; I am advancing, albeit by fits and starts, in what I can challenge myself to do, and I think raising a child may be something I—we—could handle. But, speaking for myself at any rate, I may not be ready to do so right now.

Still, I can't help remembering a poem that my mother cross-stitched and hung on our living room wall when I was a little girl in a family with seven adopted brothers and sisters. I first read these words as a child of seven or eight, and have never forgotten them:

> *Not flesh of my flesh,*
> *Nor bone of my bone,*
> *But still, miraculously, my own.*
> *Never forget, for a single minute,*
> *You weren't born under my heart,*
> *But in it.*

But now I'm 43 years old and, I'm sorry to say, the clock has not stopped ticking—it ticks ever louder. The sound threatens only to intensify over time as month by month and year by year I come ever closer to the end of possibility. I wonder whether I'll be visited by the storm and shadow of severe depression once menopause comes and time irrevocably runs out. Even now, it's getting harder and harder to sleep at night pondering my childless life; my thoughts run both to glowing "what if" fantasies and gloomy pouting.

Yes, my baby hunger keeps growing. I watch myself seek out babies in carriages being walked by parents (I never actually go up and talk to the mothers and fathers or touch the babies, but I do admire them from a distance). With something like ardor I peruse the baby picture galleries on websites like www.iVillage.com and www.AnneGeddes.com, envying the moms who can call those babies their own. Sometimes I even collect baby names in my mind, not daring to actually write them down. I wonder ruefully how it would feel to have my own little baby girl or boy lie in my arms, seek my breast and suckle (that's if I had one of my own rather than adopting, of course).

From what real-live mothers have told me and from what I have read, breast-feeding is one of the most awe-inspiring, intimate experiences it is possible to have, rivaling sexual intercourse. One mother of teenagers had obviously not forgotten her experiences many years ago—she described the sweetness of having her baby boy gaze up at her while feeding and her looking back, the two bonding to each other with their souls in their eyes, and the tug at her heart hearing his coos produced. (A lot of good that fantasy does; even if by some miracle I did or could have a baby, I could never breast-feed him or her because of all the medications that would pass into my milk and enter the baby's system.)

I've also had a recurring dream lately about doing art therapy with kids, which seems a much more practical avenue to pursuing my wish to interact with children. And sometimes I still dream that I myself am pregnant, but eventually I wake up, quite literally, to reality. Of course, I do find myself eagerly vying to spend time with my brother's and sisters' children, having many nieces and nephews who range in age from toddlerhood to young adulthood. The genuine joy and energy renewal I receive every time I visit my extended family is, mostly, devoid of jealousy that I am not in their position of having had children, whereas I know I won't. I have to admit that at times I do feel resentful that my husband and I could not follow in our respective siblings' footsteps and raise families as they did. But I am not angry at my brothers and sisters, simply at the situation.

And at least so far, I've been able simply to enjoy talking and playing with my nephews and nieces, and I often buy little toys or art supplies for them, read books and make art with them, to stay connected. I am very fortunate to have, among others in my family, an artistic goddaughter and a nephew whom I eventually would like to mentor in some sort of art therapy way (if either one shows any signs of wanting this involvement), as well as my aforementioned toddler goddaughter who has a shy and gentle yet silly way about her.

So, after more praying on my part, and reflecting and talking together about our plans, Tom and I made a final decision that we would do better by remaining childless. This was a difficult decision, and I can't say for sure that we're not just being selfish. But in another way, we're choosing the unselfish way, because we want to devote our time and energy instead to our dream project of starting a consumer arts recovery center, maybe in our retirement. It ultimately makes more sense to me to use our gifts in ways that can help many people, especially given the possibility that Tom and I would likely not have made good parents due to our mental health. But I think we will make good artists and consumer therapists.

The final consideration that shaped my decision is the well-known fact that once a couple has a child, the mother often must focus most of her energy on her child at the expense of her husband, at least when the children are young. Instead, I want Tom and me to experience life together, and in wanting him all to myself—again, call me selfish. Still, it wouldn't be fair to him to lose my love and attention.

QUEEN OF THE ROAD—?

Speaking of stretching my previous limitations: I decided in the beginning of March 2006 that I finally might be ready to learn to drive. This would involve another of the challenges of our marriage: Tom agreed to take me to deserted parking lots, and later to quiet residential streets, and practice driving with me until I felt ready to take a behind-the-wheel class.

I felt very nervous about this, naturally. The anxiety that was the first harbinger of my psychiatric problems has never fully left me; although I only occasionally experience actual panic attacks, I've been told by one psychiatrist whom I consulted that I likely meet criteria for GAD (generalized anxiety disorder). In other words, I worry irrationally about every little thing possible, much of the time, to the point that it occasionally prevents me from sleeping.

I hate to admit that I was too scared to light a match until I was 15 years old, and that to this day I often tremble at crossing highways, even with a stoplight. I even worry when we do laundry that the dryer is going to catch on fire at any moment. And I never learned to drive a car because of my unreasonable phobia of accidentally causing or being the victim of an auto accident. My stomach clenches and my heart palpitates when I ride as a passenger with my husband or a sibling—I've even suffered full-blown panic attacks while a passenger in other people's cars on a swift-moving highway, particularly at night.

Another inborn trait that has obstructed my sense of comfort around people has been my extreme sensitivity. Somewhat like people who live with PTSD, I have always had a hair-trigger startle threshold and a sense of environmental hyper-vigilance. Easily overwhelmed by ordinary stimuli around me, I become disproportionately startled and even jump out of my seat at unexpected sounds, such as people raising their voices or traffic sounds heard while crossing the street. I've often had trouble making eye contact with people because it seems too intense to bear.

In fact, now that my mood symptoms and occasional psychosis are under reasonably good control, the main problem that persists is my intermittent anxiety. Sometimes I despair of ever being able to exit the fortress of fear I hide within. My whole life seems to be ruled by my neurotic nervousness when it flares up. This extends to my entire personality or temperament, which has been since birth the aforementioned "highly reactive" type. So my illness seems to have come full circle again, back to anxiety.

Right now I don't quite see how I'll overcome this phobic nervousness, when I'm still too afraid to even turn on our Camry. I'm terrified—irrationally, I know—that if I turn the key, the car will suddenly jerk forward or backward, completely out of control. Tom assured me that this can never happen as long as the car is in park mode, but I told him I'd have to see it to believe it.

The other, much more gruesome, possibility that frightens me is the chance that I could be driving along and another car could suddenly hit me, or I could fail to react and hit someone else, and cause either their or my (or God forbid, Tom's) death! If I caused someone else to die, how could I ever live with the guilt? If Tom died, I'd want to die. And if I died, well, I wouldn't be living anymore anyway. I know I'm "disasterizing," as my psychiatrist calls it (my psychotherapist uses a similar term from cognitive therapy, "catastrophizing"), but I can't help being horrified by these nightmarish possibilities.

I suppose these are chances all drivers take every time they get out on the road, but why do most people take these chances so nonchalantly, and why can't I do the same? Maybe all that is required is a little desensitization to the driving experience. If so, I'll get a taste of this next weekend, when Tom plans to take me driving in a parking lot.

It will probably be necessary to do one of the things I do best, and use imagery to control my fears. I can start imagining myself driving on a highway and smoothly passing other cars, moving into exit lanes, and speeding up or slowing down, reacting calmly as the ever-changing traffic flow demands. I also know that, in the actual driving situation, breathing deeply and imagining warm light surrounding me while silently saying, "God, be with us" will help too. I should talk to my psychotherapist about desensitization exercises as well.

*   *   *   *

After I wrote these reflections on driving, Tom took me to an empty school parking lot near our house one weekend. And I actually drove, and even had fun! I had thought beforehand, and it turned out that he had supposed too, that all I'd be able to do was turn on the car a couple of times, in our first session.

However, I not only turned the car on and off, but also I drove it up and down the parking lot using the brake *and* the accelerator. And I practiced turning again and again, until I started to "get a feel for the way the car handles." I discovered, with Tom's instruction and my own empirical observations, that once I turn the wheel the whole way around to make a sharp U-turn, the wheel will straighten out automatically and I just have to help it a little. In my surprised words, "Oh, I can let the car do some of the work for me!" In Tom's words, "Yep, that's power steering."

I'll admit that in the beginning I was terrified. For example, I panicked when I put the car in drive (with Tom's help), took my foot off the brake, and the car naturally started moving forward. "Help! How do I stop the car?!" I implored Tom. He was, luckily, very calm while I was frightened, and just said, put your foot on the brake again, gently. I did so, and, what do you know, the car stopped (a little jerkily because I not-so-gently slammed on the brake).

After I acquainted myself with the basic workings of the car through trial and error, though, I started to enjoy myself. I varied the types and directions of turns I made, zigzagging across the parking lot, growing more assured as I proceeded. Discovering that *I* could control the car instead of having the car control me was exhilarating. Empowering, even.

I can't say enough about what a wonderful teacher/coach Tom was. He remained unfailingly relaxed and reassuring, urging me to do what I wouldn't have thought possible a mere month ago. He was endlessly patient with me as I practiced driving the same 100-yard length of parking lot for more than an hour. And when I had mentally exhausted myself for the day, Tom told me how well I had done and how he knew I would be a good driver, and how proud he is of me. I'm proud of myself too—now I can actually visualize myself driving on the highway instead of dying on the highway!

*   *   *   *

Alas, it was not to be. Some four years later, I reflect on the panic that was my downfall once I did finally take a behind-the-wheel driving class. The first instructor I had took me out on a major highway my very first time behind the wheel (outside of my lessons with Tom in our nearby parking lot). I almost screamed, I was so frightened and unmoored.

Not only did I have a full-blown anxiety attack in the car with the instructor during the two hours that seemed never to end, I proceeded to have three more panic attacks in swift succession, once when driving with a thankfully more compassionate instructor, and twice more with Tom. Tom was, of course, a very understanding driving coach, but one thing he did not have—that even the least compassionate driving instructor did have—was dual controls. So I felt intensely powerless in the car and had to turn into the nearest driveway rather than go any further after only driving about half of a mile.

I finally decided that I would concede defeat and give up on learning to drive, at least for now. All those anxiety attacks just weren't worth it, and at any rate, I now participate in a carpool that gets me to and from work, giving me door-to-door service. As I see it, I'm paying not only for the rides to work, but also for peace of mind. Maybe I'll learn to drive in Tom's and my retirement; maybe I never will. But driving seems secondary to all my other plans in life, like writing this book, becoming a licensed counselor and art therapist, and maybe starting or working with a mental health/arts nonprofit. You just have to pick your battles.

MANIA OR AMBITION?

I've recently finished reading young bipolar dynamo Lizzie Simon's book *Detour: My Bipolar Road Trip in 4-D*. I am amazed at her accomplishments as a theater producer and writer by the age of 22 or 23. When I was that age, I'd just graduated from college and was about to land in the hospital again.

However, she and I and, I suspect, many other people who have bipolar disorder share the trait of dreaming big dreams. When I neared the end of my graduate studies in art therapy in 2000, I developed the idea of moving to New Mexico after graduation to pursue clinical work in artsy Santa Fe or Albuquerque, surrounded by the desert's otherworldly colors.

My aforementioned ambition was to build an artist's colony or center (for all types of performing and fine arts) where people with mental illnesses could gather and work/play with their peers. This would be a consumer—or peer—operated center where even the treatment professionals would be people living with such illnesses, because I strongly believe in the consumer-provider model of psychiatric rehabilitation. And I would be the founder, director, and one of the art therapists.

Obviously, this dream hasn't been realized—yet, anyway. But I do want to actualize that ambition in some form, at some point in the future, maybe after I've retired from government service. Tom supports me fully in this endeavor, and will help me with it when the time comes. And we may end up living in Santa Fe or maybe, by turns, Philadelphia (PA) or even Sacramento (CA) by then—all locations we've enjoyed visiting on relaxing vacations.

So, my fancy idea about starting my own consumer arts center, maybe in a locale across the country, when in reality I know nothing about running a business and suspect I would be ill-suited for administrative work . . . As the chapter title posits, is this manic grandiosity or a realizable vision?

I think that's an important dilemma; it begs the question of whether the bold ideas of many people living with bipolar disorder are laudable outgrowths of their native personalities, or merely artifacts of a brain disease.

Who can say? It's true that when I'm anxious-manic my mind swims with possibilities for new jobs for me and Tom; graduate programs for us to pursue; kids to adopt; writing grants for me to secure; new neighborhoods to move to—all of which seem imperative *right now.*

And as I said, I'm not the only one with racing thoughts that might actually be productive. In his manic states (or were they?), Tom has written drafts of autobiographical plays, painted a brilliantly colored mural on the wall of an apartment he owned in Baltimore, planned to sell his original drawings and photos on eBay. Personally, I don't think Tom's ideas were merely flights of fancy—I respect the urges behind his aspirations and believe in his core of talent. And he believes in mine.

Not to mention the bipolar artists, writers, musicians, statesmen of the past and present who have enriched our world more than I ever could. I'm in good company as a creative person with this illness, as medical researchers such as Kay Redfield Jamison and Nancy Andreasen are discovering. People like Vincent van Gogh, Patty Duke, Robert Schumann, Abraham Lincoln, Robin Williams, Winston Churchill, Virginia Woolf—all could be viewed either as the cultural and political touchstones that they are, or as people whose rash imaginations and moody temperaments ran away with themselves.

The people I've just named changed the world through their gifts; mine are considerably lesser. Still, it boils down to the tapestry whose weft is personality and whose warp is illness. It is so difficult to separate the threads that have been intertwined so closely. Maybe genius (or at least some degree of creativity or fluidity of thinking) and madness are often bedfellows, as the saying goes.

Well, this problem is interesting to speculate about, and Tom and I found after we met that we each had copies of Kay Redfield Jamison's *Touched With Fire,* which describes famous artists whose creative productivity cycled with their moods. But real life, for us bipolar non-celebrities, is a different story.

In real life, when I begin to speak excitedly about lots of grand ideas, I automatically wonder whether I'm going manic, and so does my doctor. And I don't know whether to trust these bright ideas zinging through my mind—or simply write them off as poorly conceptualized reminders that I ought to just calm down, slow down, stop worrying, take things one step at a time.

I think all too often, clinicians—and, sadly, people with bipolar disorder ourselves—discredit the wonderful contributions we can and do make to society. Maybe people like Lincoln and van Gogh and Woolf wouldn't have been so gifted and influential had they not been emotionally sensitive in the way that people who live with our illness are. Maybe my own desire to paint and write wouldn't be as intense if all that was driving it was modest talent, instead of modest talent coupled with swinging vicissitudes of emotion.

I find it incredibly difficult to separate basic personality from symptoms of a mental illness, both in myself and in other consumers I know. Everyone, including people who've never been bipolar, has ups and downs. But in someone like me, is an "up" a temporary good mood sprung from a happy event; the manifestation of a cheerful temperament; or a harbinger of impending mania? Likewise, is a "down" brought on by a disappointing personal setback; by a slight natural bent toward pessimism (which some clinicians are beginning to think is itself a symptom of low-grade dysthymia); or by imminent severe depression?

Similarly, is it necessary to medicate away every mood swing? How do I (and my doctor) know when to aggressively treat emerging mood symptoms, and when to simply roll with the circumstances life brings me? It seems my proverbial glass is nearly always either completely full or completely empty!

For instance, as I wrote an earlier version of this in April 2006, my husband and I awaited the results of our life insurance physicals, which included HIV testing, to see how high our premiums would be. We were still trying to decide whether to adopt a child, and if so, when in the next few years. Tom had applied for a new job, but he hadn't been contacted by the person who interviewed him yet. I was anxiously awaiting news of a potential promotion in my current position.

Needless to say, trying to resolve all of these situations took its toll on us. For me in particular, waiting and indeterminacy are agonizing and quite stressful. When faced with such circumstances, I'm more emotionally labile and high-strung even than normal, and my anxiety is quick to surface and slow to ebb.

I haven't been able to figure out whether, at such times, I'm simply feeling the stress any normal person would in my situation, or whether I'm decompensating back into a period of rapid cycling. In other words, should I put up and shut up, or should I seek help for potential destabilization? The best answer seems to be to deal with the stress as best I can with help from Tom and my psychotherapist and spiritual practice, but to call my psychiatrist if symptoms increase. At the same time, I believe we should feel free to pursue our goals with all the dedication we can afford to them.

And so, back in May 2006, Tom and I met with my mom a couple of times and discussed with her in some detail our plans for a consumer-run or at least consumer-friendly arts center in Albuquerque. To our surprise, she was incredibly supportive and expressed an interest in helping us research options and write a business plan, or connect with an existing organization, perhaps in some other location in the United States if the need for consumer participation in the arts is already being met in New Mexico. Mom has lots of connections out there through past work in the mental health field and her current work at Columbia University, and graciously offered to talk to people she knows in hopes of helping us realize our dream.

When our Albuquerque arts center seemed to become more of a realizable goal rather than a mere pipe-dream, I temporarily changed directions in terms of further education. For a few weeks I gathered information about graduate-level certificates in nonprofit management, believing Tom and I could end up founding our own nonprofit organization in Albuquerque for consumers to participate in fine and performing arts. However, as I didn't see myself as the administrative type, knowing that my talents and interests lie more in the arts and in therapy, my plans again changed.

As taxing as working toward my art therapy degree became at times, the recollection hasn't hindered me from recently discovering that I wanted to go back to school (again)—but not for management or business education. My calling, since I was 17 and newly recovered from depression, has always been to help people who have serious mental illnesses on a direct, personal basis. Even if I may not prove to be able to do so full-time. At one point recently, I considered obtaining a master's of social work from the University of Maryland, with the eventual goal of treating people like me in a part-time private practice, while at the same time maintaining my research/recruitment full-time job in the schizophrenia research branch of NIMH. (Meanwhile, I began investigating grants and scholarships because I'm already $30,000 in debt, having financed my art therapy degree completely through student loans.) I originally planned, once I completed my degree on a part-time basis, which should have taken four years, to return to federal government work as a social worker, perhaps in the same research branch at NIMH where I currently work, or perhaps for another branch or agency at the U.S. Department of Health and Human Services. This course of events, it seemed, would form a neat circle leading me from psychiatric patient to psychiatric provider.

However, I finally decided to go back to school, not for a social work degree, but to Johns Hopkins University for a post-master's certificate in mental health counseling—to obtain the 60 graduate credits necessary to gain licensure as a clinical professional counselor in Maryland. My main interest is in helping people with mental illnesses rather than serving the wide range of populations that a social worker would, and I believed counseling would narrow my focus accordingly. Furthermore, most of the credits I needed could be taken at a Johns Hopkins campus in Montgomery County close to our home, at night or on weekends. At Johns Hopkins, I took the requisite 12 classes over the course of two years (from 2007 to 2009) to receive my certificate.

I knew going back to school would provide some degree of stress, but when I actually did begin courses for my counseling certificate at John Hopkins, I proved myself prepared to handle it, since I felt relatively sane and balanced. Not that this other stint in graduate school passed with no challenges or mood swings—such is the nature of bipolar disorder! Yet, I finished my coursework with flying colors.

Still, during my days at Johns Hopkins, what did I do but make the same "mistake" (or perhaps ill-thought-out decision) that I did during my art therapy program, all over again. Once again I disclosed my bipolar status in several classes, and now I'm not sure what, if any, good this did—except possibly to expose classmates to a (hopefully) "regular" person who was successfully living with a mental illness. I'm now apt to scorn myself for this decision—was I at base simply trying to elicit attention or admiration because I secretly felt inadequate as a counselor and wanted to be granted a handicap, a special exception, in case I made mistakes (as invariably I did)?

And because of my engulfing fear of making errors or being less than perfect, before settling on the goal of getting a graduate degree in counseling, I briefly considered following the long route and getting my Ph.D. in clinical psychology from the University of Maryland at College Park, which has a predoctoral schizophrenia research training program as a component of its doctoral clinical psychology program. I wondered whether this terminal degree might afford me the best opportunity to make a difference in the lives of other people with mental illnesses, since I already have a 19-year career in schizophrenia research and recruitment.

After investigating various Ph.D. programs in clinical psychology in the greater Washington area, and finding out that full-time attendance is necessary to earn the degree, though, I decided that the Johns Hopkins counseling program, which would allow me to study part-time, would be more feasible. And a counseling degree made more sense for me anyway, because, if I'm honest with myself, I'm much more clinically oriented than research-oriented. Tom supports me fully in this desire for further education, and he believes I'd be best at individual therapy with people living with mental illnesses.

I concur. But first I'll have to learn to control my easy tears when confronted with clients' problems, my over-identification with them, my need to be liked by my clients, my need to fix everything for them, and my lack of comfort with negative affect. Actually, it seems I've got quite a few stumbling-blocks to overcome on the road to readying myself to counsel others.

With this recognition, I recently took the plunge into post-graduate provision of therapy. From September through December 2009 I participated in a counseling internship with patients undergoing treatment for alcohol and drug addiction at NIAAA (the National Institute on Alcohol Abuse and Alcoholism). Under the outstanding supervision of a compassionate and no-nonsense licensed counselor and nurse, I co-facilitated cognitive behavioral therapy groups, women's groups, and multi-family sessions, and assisted in running a weekly clinic for outpatients with addictions. At one point I was privileged to work with a client on an individual basis, bringing some of my art therapy skills into play.

However, working as a substance abuse counselor almost led me to give up all my dreams of developing into a bona fide art therapist and counselor. My problem was that I kept on crying while attempting to deliver treatment! Because I've had some contact in my personal life with others who have addiction problems, tears kept welling up whenever I tried to assist with a group, and especially whenever I worked with my individual client. While my supervisor was forgiving of these tendencies and in fact counseled me that this emotional overload would most likely subside in time, I was not forgiving of myself. I concluded for some months that I simply was not cut out to be a counselor at all—maybe not even an art therapist.

I give thanks that I worked on this issue sufficiently with my own psychotherapist that I once again determined that because counseling and art therapy have for some time been part of my picture of myself, I should pursue these goals. Maybe I won't seek out substance abuse counseling positions, but, knowing that I have always felt comfortable and fairly level-headed around people with schizophrenia or mood and anxiety disorders, I feel I could successfully work in a verbal therapy or art therapy modality with them. If I do want to be an effective counselor, I need to work my hardest to learn the necessary skills. I owe it to all the people who are going to need my help.

In a few weeks I'll take the National Counseling Exam to gain certification as an LGPC (licensed graduate professional counselor), and after that I can start pursuing the 2,000 hours of client counseling contact necessary, along with 200 hours of clinical supervision, to become an LCPC (licensed clinical professional counselor). At that level, I'll be able to practice independently. And even right now, new opportunities may be opening up for me: eight federal positions as readjustment counseling therapists with the Veterans Health Administration have been announced, and an art therapist position right at NIH where I currently work is scheduled to open in the next week. Of course, I will apply for all of these jobs.

I've also recently taken a stab at doctoral education after all, although I withdrew after one class. I know now that I was largely motivated to enter an online psychology Ph.D. program because of my shame over not having achieved enough—meaning that I felt in awe of colleagues who held Ph.D.s, like professors or art therapy contacts, and imagined that I would not be "good enough" unless I too attained a Ph.D. At the time, however, I convinced myself that I could handle the work and that the degree would be absolutely necessary for me to maintain basic self-esteem.

As it happens, I was able to handle working full-time and studying one class at a time. I consistently received A grades for my assignments and as a final grade for the introductory class I completed. But I discovered that my program was not accredited by the American Psychological Association (which isn't surprising, considering the classes were all delivered in an online format and there were no residency requirements), and that I was essentially wasting money by continuing with the program, despite the fact that I had enjoyed the class I'd completed.

As well, I've reached a tentative understanding with myself that maybe I can still be happy and worth as much as anyone else I know, even without a Ph.D.! I know that I can pursue doctoral work again in my retirement, should the dream revisit me. One of the most essential lessons I've gleaned from my graduate academic programs and the resultant client-centered therapy I've administered is that it's all right to slow down! I don't need to become a Ph.D. psychologist, along with the world's most brilliant counselor and art therapist, by yesterday. The people with whom I work will probably benefit much more from my efforts if I take a relaxed and compassionate, rather than an anxious and intensely over-achieving, attitude toward them and the intimate words and creations we share.

CONCLUSION: SOMEDAY IS NOW

For better or worse, I am as wedded to my bipolar disorder as I am wedded to Tom. And to echo Kay Redfield Jamison's thoughts in her autobiography *An Unquiet Mind,* this is a union I would not sever even if I could.

I did not choose to have bipolar illness, but, having it, I would not choose to be rid of it. A friend of mine recently spoke pityingly of the "years I'd lost" due to my illness, chiefly referring to the crippling depressions. Surprised, I told her that I didn't consider my dark years, even those of my rather tortured adolescence, to be "wasted" or "lost" at all.

As Benjamin Franklin said, "That which hurts, instructs." Any pain I've experienced through depression, mania, anxiety, or psychosis has been more than compensated for by the growth it has brought me. I've gained strength of character, clarity of purpose, and most importantly, depth of love and compassion. All of these qualities have led me to my calling to help others like me with mental illnesses.

I know I will learn to be an empathic counselor and art therapist because I have walked—sometimes crawled—the road my fellow travelers may be just setting forth on. And if I have survived, maybe I can help them do the same. Maybe we will never be "normal"—but the world will still be the better for our having walked this path.

"Someday," I dreamed as I first recovered, I'd help others as I'd been helped. Someday is now, in everything I do and everyone whose life I touch. I hope I've touched yours as you have read this book.